THE EASIEST DUTCH OVEN COOKBOOK 2021

Cook Delicious Recipes with Your Whole Family

CONTENTS

Chapter 3

BEEF AND PORK

Chapter 1

INTRODUCTION

There are many kitchen gadgets and pots that you need to have in your Kitchen. Some will help you cook faster or slower while some are designed specifically for a particular type of food. It's essential to have some of these gadgets in your kitchen.

However, you need to consider buying some gadgets that can help you achieve many things in order to cut cost and save space in your kitchen. One of these gadgets that help you live a minimalist life is Dutch oven. Dutch oven is one of the most versatile cookware one can ever have. With its cast iron body or enameled cast iron body, you can use it to cook on different heating surfaces like coal, wood, stove top, or oven. It can be used anywhere and can be used to cook any type of food.

Moreover, it is highly durable and can serve you for ages. In my house I still use Dutch oven that my grand mother bought in her youthful age. That's how long it can go.

Other things that will make you consider using Dutch oven for all your cooking are;

They Save Energy: Dutch ovens have high heat retention capacity which makes it ideal for those that want to save energy and cut cost. Even after turning the oven off, your Dutch oven will continue cooking which helps to save energy.

They Are Safe: Unlike some non-stick cookware that are coated with chemicals, Dutch oven is mostly made with cast iron.

Choosing The Right Dutch Oven

As a beginner it might be overwhelming to figure out the type of Dutch oven to buy. There are many sizes, colors, and styles of Dutch oven to choose from. Though Dutch oven can serve you in many ways, but choosing the right type that suits your need will make you enjoy Dutch oven the more. If your aim is to get a Dutch oven for outdoor cooking and camping, there are specific Dutch ovens for that purpose. Serving size is also an important factor in deciding the Dutch oven to buy.

Thus, choosing the right Dutch oven to serve you best depends on many factors. However, there are certain questions that can help you decide the perfect Dutch oven for you. Answers to the following questions will make the decision process easy for you.

What Size Of Dutch Oven Should You Buy?

There are various sizes of Dutch oven out there and they serve different purpose. Though Dutch oven is highly versatile and can be used for so many dishes, it is best practice to use the correct pot for your cooking. Thus, deciding on the best Dutch oven to use comes down to factors like the type of food you are cooking and the number of people your are cooking for.

This takes us further to answering questions like;

What Type Of Food Do You Cook?

You need to consider this question because different foods and cooking techniques require specific type of pot or pan and space. So, is the pot for roasts and braises, or are you planning to use it mostly for soup and stew? This is important to take into consideration. For instance, your stew or soup will need pot with tall side. Much width is not needed in this case, but braising and roasting require a wider Dutch oven so that its space can facilitate effective browning and caramelizing.

How Many People Do You Cook For?

When it comes to size of Dutch oven to use or buy, there is a general rule of thumb that will guide you to make the best decision – one quart per person. People consider this to be the serving size, it's fine as long as it serves the purpose right.

So, if you are cooking for 5 persons, it means that you should consider using a minimum of 5-quart Dutch oven. For that servings of 5, using a Dutch oven with 6 to 7 quarts capacity would be ideal.

You may also consider if you like cooking so you have leftovers. With this, you may consider adding more quarts to the budget to help you stay flexible in your kitchen. However, if you are considering buying Dutch oven bigger than 7 quarts, you have to ensure that it will comfortably enter in your oven.

Types of Dutch Oven

We have considered factors like size and type of food when choosing the right Dutch oven for your cooking. Those are the basics, but to move further, you need to determine whether you are buying enameled cast iron Dutch oven or solid cast iron Dutch oven.

Enameled Cast Iron Dutch Oven:

When your traditional cast iron Dutch oven is enameled it cannot be used for camping where you use campfire for cooking. However, its durability is still in tact, and it is an excellent choice for home cooking as they heat more evenly than the solid cast iron Dutch oven. Moreover, you do not need to season the pot again. You can get this type of Dutch oven in variety of colors and they add to your kitchen decor.

Buying Tip: Go for quality ones that are rated for high heat/temperature.

Solid Cast Iron Dutch Oven:

These are the most versatile of Dutch ovens – best for campfire and can also be used at home at a very high temperature. However, you need to season the Dutch oven to add that bit of extra maintenance.

Whether enameled or not, you need to purchase a quality Dutch oven so you can enjoy its versatility and durability. To get a quality Dutch oven ensure you look out for the following features:

- The Dutch oven must be made of cast iron (and covered with enamel).
- The Dutch oven must have even thickness all over.
- The Dutch oven must be rated for high temperature.

Chapter 2

BREAKFAST AND BRUNCH

Cheesy Bacon With Eggs

Total Time: 65 minutes; Prep Time: 40 minutes; Cook Time: 25 minutes
Servings: 8

Ingredients

- Bacon strips (chopped) - 1 pound
- Refrigerated o'brien hash brown potatoes - 1 package (20 ounces)
- Large eggs - 8
- Half-and-half cream - 1/2 cup
- Hot pepper sauce - 1/2 - 1 teaspoon (optional)
- Cheddar-monterey jack cheese (shredded) - 2 cups

Instructions

1. Using 36 charcoal briquettes, prepare your grill to medium-high heat. You can use wood chips.
2. Add the bacon to your Dutch oven and cook over the fire until it becomes crispy. Stir occasionally.
3. Remove from heat and drain with a paper towel. Reserve 2 tablespoons of the drippings and discard the remaining.
4. Add the potatoes and press it onto the bottom of the Dutch oven.
5. Whisk the cream, egg, and pepper sauce in a bowl until the mixture blends well.
6. Pour the mixture over the potatoes. Sprinkle the bacon and cheese on top.
7. Cover the Dutch oven.
8. Once the briquettes are covered with ash, place the pot on top of 16 to 18 briquettes. Place another 16 to 18 briquettes on the cover.

9. Cook for about 25 minutes, or until the cheese is melted with the egg completely set.

10. Once done, remove from heat and serve.

Nutrition Fact

Calories: 393 | Protein: 21g | Carbohydrates: 17g | Fiber: 2g | Sugar: 2g | Fat: 25g

Grilled Shrimp And Chorizo Paella

Total Time: 30 minutes; Prep Time: 20 minutes; Cook Time: 10 minutes
Servings: 8

Ingredients

- Medium sweet red pepper (chopped) - 1
- Medium onion (chopped) - 1
- Olive oil - 2 tablespoons
- Instant brown rice - 4 cups
- Garlic (minced) – 4 cloves
- Chipotle pepper in adobo sauce (chopped) - 1
- Low-sodium chicken broth - 6 cups
- Diced tomatoes (no-salt-added) - 1 can (14-1/2 ounces)
- Saffron threads - 1 teaspoon (or use 4 teaspoons of ground turmeric)
- Medium shrimp (peeled, deveined, and uncooked) - 1 pound
- Chorizo chicken sausage (fully cooked, cut into 1/4-inch slices) - 1 package (12 ounces)
- Medium mango (coarsely chopped) - 1
- Lime juice - 2 tablespoons
- Cayenne pepper - 1/4 teaspoon
- Medium lime (cut into wedges) - 1
- Fresh cilantro (minced) - 2 tablespoons

Instructions

1. Add the red pepper and onion in your Dutch oven and saute in oil until it becomes tender.
2. Add the rice, chipotle pepper, and garlic. Saute for about 2 minutes.

3. Add the tomatoes, broth, and saffron, and bring mixture to a boil.
4. Reduce and cover the pot. Simmer for about 5 minutes or until the liquid is fully absorbed. Let it stand for 5 minutes.
5. Meanwhile, mix the mango, shrimp, and chicken sausage in a bowl.
6. Sprinkle over with the cayenne and lime juice.
7. Transfer mixture to a grill wok.
8. Cover and grill for about 8 minutes over medium heat. Stir occasionally.
9. Add the mixture to the Dutch oven and toss to combine well.
10. Garnish with the cilantro and lime wedges.
11. Serve.

Nutrition Fact

Calories: 388 | Protein: 24g | Carbohydrates: 55g | Fiber: 4g | Sugar: 11g | Fat: 9g

Red Wine Steamed Leeks

Total Time: 20 minutes

Servings: 6

Ingredients

- Medium leeks (only the white portion, halved lengthwise, and cleaned) - 6
- Large tomato (chopped) - 1
- Small navel orange (peeled and sectioned, and chopped) - 1
- Fresh parsley (minced) - 2 tablespoons
- Greek olives (sliced) - 2 tablespoons
- Capers (drained) - 1 teaspoon
- Red wine vinegar - 1 teaspoon
- Olive oil - 1 teaspoon
- Grated orange zest - 1/2 teaspoon
- Pepper - 1/2 teaspoon
- Crumbled feta cheese

Instructions

1. Place a steamer basket over 1 inch of water in your Dutch oven.
2. Place the leeks in the basket and bring the water to a boil.
3. Lower the heat to maintain a low boil.
4. Cover and steam for about 10 minutes or until it becomes tender.
5. Meanwhile, add other ingredients in a bowl.
6. Transfer the cooked leeks onto your serving bowl.
7. Top with the tomato mixture and cheese.
8. Serve.

Nutrition Fact

Calories: 83 | Protein: 2g | Carbohydrates: 16g | Fiber: 3g | Sugar: 6g |
Fat: 2g

Spicy Pear Risotto

Total Time: 50 minutes; Prep Time: 15 minutes; Cook Time: 35 minutes
Servings: 10

Ingredients

- Chicken broth - 6 cups
- Sweet onion (finely chopped) - 1/2 cup
- Sweet red pepper (finely chopped) - 1/2 cup
- Garlic (minced) – 1 clove
- Butter - 3 tablespoons
- Arborio rice (uncooked) - 3 cups
- Chinese five-spice powder - 1/2 teaspoon
- Cayenne pepper – a dash
- Apple cider (or juice) - 1/4 cup
- Large pear (peeled & chopped) - 1
- Grated Parmesan cheese (divided) - 1/2 cup
- Pepper (coarsely ground) - 1/2 teaspoon
- Chives (chopped) optional

Instructions

1. Add the broth to your saucepan and heat. Keep it warm.
2. Add the oil, red pepper, onion, and garlic to your Dutch oven. Saute for about 3 minutes or until it becomes tender.
3. Stir in the five-spice powder, rice, and cayenne. Cook for about 3 minutes. Stir frequently.
4. Set the heat to medium and add the apple cider.

5. Stir and cook until the liquid is absorbed completely.
6. Add the warm birth and stir constantly.
7. Cook until the risotto becomes creamy, about 25 minutes.
8. Stir in the pepper, pear, and ¼ cup of cheese.
9. Cook until the mixture heats through.
10. Sprinkle over with the remaining cheese.
11. Top with chives and serve.

Nutrition Fact

Calories: 293 | Protein: 6g | Carbohydrates: 54g | Fiber: 2g | Sugar: 4g | Fat: 5g

Tangy Bacon Baked Beans

Total Time: 1 hour 20 minutes; Prep Time: 20 minutes; Cook Time: 60 minutes

Servings: 18

Ingredients

- Bacon strips (chopped) - 1 pound
- Large onion (chopped) - 1
- Large sweet yellow pepper (chopped) - 1
- Large sweet red pepper (chopped) - 1
- Garlic (minced) – 6 cloves
- Chipotle pepper (ground) - 1 teaspoon
- Pepper - 1/2 teaspoon
- Pork and beans - 2 cans (15 ounces each)
- Butter beans (rinsed & drained) - 1 can (16 ounces)
- Kidney beans (rinsed & drained) - 1 can (16 ounces)
- Black-eyed peas (rinsed & drained) - 1 can (15½ ounces)
- Garbanzo beans (rinsed & drained) - 1 can (15 ounces)
- Pinto beans (rinsed & drained) - 1 can (15 ounces)
- Black beans (rinsed & drained) - 1 can (15 ounces)
- Barbecue sauce - 2 bottles (18 ounces each)
- Cider vinegar - 1/3 cup
- Liquid smoke - 1 tablespoon (optional)

Instructions

1. Preheat your oven to 350F.

2. Add the bacon in your Dutch and cook over medium heat until it becomes crisp. Stir occasionally.
3. Remove from the pot and drain with paper towels.
4. Add the garlic, onion, red pepper, yellow pepper, pepper, and chipotle pepper to the pot and cook in the drippings until the veggies become tender. Remove from heat.
5. Add the cook bacon and the beans to the pot.
6. Stir in the vinegar, BBQ sauce, and liquid smoke.
7. Cover the pot and bake for about 1 hour.

Nutrition Fact

Calories: 369 | Protein: 13g | Carbohydrates: 56g | Fiber: 9g | Sugar: 24g | Fat: 11g

Chili and Cheese Casserole

Servings: 6

Ingredients

- Lean hamburger - 1 lb.
- Corn chips - 1.5 cups
- Cheddar cheese (grated) - 1 cup
- Chili - 1 can
- Onion (chopped) - 1 quarter

Instructions

1. Heat your Dutch oven to 350F.
2. Add the hamburger and onion to the pot. Cook and crumble until it turns browns.
3. Add the chili and stir. Bring mixture to a boil.
4. Stir and simmer for 5 minutes.
5. Add the corn chips and stir.
6. Top with the cheese and cover the pot.
7. Bake at 350F for about 20 minutes.

Red Potato Cod Chowder

Total Time: 45 minutes

Servings: 6

Ingredients

- Extra-virgin olive oil - 3 tablespoons
- Onion (diced) - 1 cup
- Celery (diced) - 1 cup
- All-purpose flour - ½ cup
- Worcestershire sauce - 1 tablespoon
- Old bay seasoning (low-sodium) - ¾ teaspoon
- Salt - ¼ teaspoon
- Pepper (ground) - ¼ teaspoon
- Fish stock (reduced-sodium) - 4 cups
- Whole milk - 1 cup
- Red potatoes (diced) - 3 cups
- Green beans (chopped) - 2 cups
- Alaskan cod (chopped into 1" Pieces) - 1 pound
- Fresh dill (chopped) – 1 (for garnish)
- Plum tomatoes (chopped) - 1 (for garnish)

Instructions

1. Add the oil to your Dutch oven and heat over medium heat.
2. Stir in the onion and celery. Stir and cook for 5 minutes.
3. Add the flour, old bay seasoning, pepper, Worcestershire, and salt.
4. Stir and cook for 1 minute.

5. Add the milk and fish stock. Stir constantly and bring the mixture to a boil.
6. Stir in the green beans, and potatoes. Bring mixture to a simmer.
7. Simmer for about 15 minutes or until the potatoes become tender.
8. Stir in the cod. Stir and cook for 4 minutes.
9. Serve.

Nutrition Fact

Calories: 270 | Protein: 18.6g | Carbohydrates: 29.1g | Fiber: 3.2g | Fat: 8.9g

Beans Rice And Peas

Total Time: 1 hour 45 minutes; Prep Time: 1 hour 20 minutes; Cook Time: 20 minutes

Servings: 8

Ingredients

- Dried red kidney beans (rinsed & drained) - 1 cup
- Low-sodium chicken stock - 6½ cups
- Parboiled rice (uncooked, rinsed, and drained) - 2 cups
- Grace pure creamed coconut (grated) - 1/4 cup
- Fresh thyme - 3 sprigs
- Habanero pepper - 1
- Kosher salt - 1/2 tsp
- Ground allspice - 1/4 tsp

Instructions

1. Add the beans and 4 cups of chicken stock in your Dutch oven, cover and soak overnight.
2. Bring the mixture to a boil and cook for 15 minutes.
3. Low the heat to medium-low and simmer for about 1 hour, or until the beans becomes tender.
4. Stir in the remaining stock and bring it to a boil.
5. Add the creamed coconut, habanero, allspice, rice, and salt. Stir and cover the pot.
6. Lower the heat to low and cook for about 20 minutes, or until the rice becomes tender.

7. Remove from heat and allow it to stand for 7 minutes.

8. Remove the habanero and thyme, and fluff rice.

9. Separate the grains and serve.

Nutrition Fact

Calories: 329 | Protein: 13g | Carbohydrates: 55g | Fiber: 4g | Sugar: 1g | Fat: 5g

Spicy Kabocha Chicken Soup

Servings: 4

Ingredients

- Spicy chicken stock
- Kabocha squash - 1 (2-pound)
- Thin wedges mixed cabbages - 4 cups
- Cooked chicken - 4 cups
- Kosher salt
- Pepper (freshly ground)
- Jalapeño (thinly sliced) - 1
- Chili oil, cilantro leaves with tender stems, and basil leaves (for serving)
- Piece ginger (peeled, finely grated) - 1 (2-inch)
- Limes (cut into wedges) – 3

Instructions

1. Add the stock to your Dutch oven and heat over medium heat.
2. Meanwhile, cut the squash into four equal wedges and remove the seeds.
3. Divide the wedges into four pieces.
4. Add the squash to the pot and simmer for about 10 minutes, until it becomes tender.
5. Add the cooked chicken and cabbage and cook for 4 minutes to heat through.
6. Transfer the soul to your serving bowls and top with the basil and jalapeno
7. Drizzle over with the chili oil and sprinkle with pinch of ginger.

8. Serve with the lime wedges

Pasta Peas Alfredo

Total Time: 25 minutes

Servings: 4

Ingredients

- Bow tie pasta (uncooked) - 3 cups
- Frozen peas - 2 cups
- Cooked medium shrimp (peeled, deveined, tails removed) - 1 pound
- Alfredo sauce - 1 jar (15 ounces)
- Parmesan cheese (shredded) - 1/4 cup

Instructions

1. Prepare the pasta following the instructions on the package.
2. Add the peas to the pasta in the last 3 minutes of cooking. Remove from heat, and drain.
3. Stir in the sauce and shrimp. Cook until it heats through. Stir occasionally.
4. Sprinkle over with the cheese.

Nutrition Fact

Calories: 545 | Protein: 41g | Carbohydrates: 60g | Fiber: 6g | Sugar: 5g | Fat: 16g

Spicy Tofu Hotpot

Total Time: 30 minutes

Servings: 6

Ingredients

- Garlic (minced) - 6 cloves
- Canola oil - 4 ounces 2 teaspoons
- Brown sugar - 1 tablespoon
- Firm tofu (water-packed) - 4 cups 14 ounces
- Low-sodium soy sauce - ¼ cup
- Chile-garlic sauce - 2 teaspoons
- Tender bok choy greens (thinly sliced) - 4 cups
- Fresh chinese-style noodles - 8 ounces
- Fresh cilantro (chopped) - ½ cup
- Vegetable broth - 14 ounces 4 cups
- Fresh shiitake mushrooms (stemmed & sliced) - 2 cups
- Grated fresh ginger - 2 tablespoons

Instructions

1. Drain the tofu and rinse it. Par dry with paper towels and cut into 1" cubes.
2. Add the oil to your Dutch oven and heat over medium heat.
3. Add garlic and ginger. Stir and cook for a minute.
4. Stir in the mushrooms and cook for about 3 minutes until they becomes soft.
5. Add the soy sauce, sugar, chile-garlic sauce, broth, and sugar.

6. Cover the pot and bring mixture to a boil.
7. Stir in the tofu and bok choy. Cover the pot and simmer for 2 minutes until the greens wilt.
8. Increase the heat to high.
9. Add the noodles and submerge in the broth.
10. Cook for 3 minutes until the noodles become tender.
11. Remove the pot from heat and stir in the cilantro.
12. Serve.

Nutrition Fact

Calories: 214 | Protein: 12.3g | Carbohydrates: 30.9g | Fiber: 3.9g | Fat: 5.4g

Mushroom Spaghetti

Total Time: 35 minutes; Prep Time: 10 minutes; Cook Time: 25 minutes
Servings: 4

Ingredients

- Ground beef (90% lean) - 1 pound
- Fresh mushrooms (sliced) – 1¾ cups
- Tomato juice - 3 cups
- Diced tomatoes (no salt added, drained) - 1 can (14½ ounces)
- Tomato sauce (no salt added) - 1 can (8 ounces)
- Dried minced onion - 1 tablespoon
- Salt - 1/2 teaspoon
- Garlic powder - 1/2 teaspoon
- Mustard (ground) - 1/2 teaspoon
- Pepper - 1/4 teaspoon
- Allspice (ground) - 1/8 teaspoon
- Mace (ground) - 1/8 teaspoon (optional)
- Multigrain spaghetti (uncooked, cut into pieces) - 6 ounces
- Shaved Parmesan cheese (optional)

Instructions

1. Add the beef and mushrooms to your Dutch oven and cook over medium heat until the meat changes color. Break it into crumbles and drain.
2. Add the tomatoes, tomato juice, tomato sauce, seasonings, and onion.
3. Bring mixture to a boil.

4. Add the spaghetti and stir.
5. Cover the out and simmer for about 15 minutes or until the spaghetti becomes tender.
6. Serve with the cheese.

Nutrition Fact

Calories: 414 | Protein: 33g | Carbohydrates: 48g | Fiber: 6g | Sugar: 15g | Fat: 10g

Creamy Sausage Balls

Makes: 12 balls

Ingredients

- Butter - 1/4 cup
- Bulk sausage - 1lb.
- Egg - 1
- Cheddar cheese (grated) - 6oz.
- Bisquick mix – 3 cups
- Hot pepper sauce (optional)

Instructions

1. Add the butter to your Dutch oven and heat to 350F.
2. Add all ingredients in a bowl and mix thoroughly with your hands.
3. Form 1" balls with the mixture.
4. Place the balls in the pot and bake for about 15 minutes.
5. Transfer to your serving bowls and sprinkle with hot sauce.

Tomato Bean Chili

Total Time: 2 hours 10 minutes; Prep Time: 10 minutes; Cook Time: 2 hours
Servings: 6

Ingredients

- Stew meat (cut into ¾" Cubes) - 1½ pounds
- Kosher salt – to taste
- Black pepper (freshly ground) - to taste
- Red onion (diced) - 1
- Garlic (minced) - 4 cloves
- Jalapeños (minced) - 1-3
- Tomatoes (diced) - 1 (14.5-ounce) can
- Tomato sauce - 1 (8-ounce) can
- Chili powder - 2 tablespoons
- Kidney beans (drained & rinsed) - 2 (15-ounce) cans
- For serving use shredded jalapeño cheese, and jalapeño cornbread

Instructions

1. Season the stew meat with pepper, and salt.
2. Add the oil to your Dutch oven and heat over medium-high heat.
3. Add the seasoned meat and sear for about 2 minutes, or until it turns brown.
4. Add the garlic, onion, and jalapenos and cook for 2 minutes.
5. Stir in the tomato sauce, tomatoes, kidney beans, chili powder, and 1 cup of water (or more).

6. Cover the pot, lower the heat to low and simmer until the meat becomes tender, about 1 ½ - 2 hours.
7. Serve with the cornbread and jalapeno cheese.

Cinnamon Cranberry Punch

Total Time: 30 minutes

Makes: 25.5 cups

Ingredients

- Fresh cranberries - 4 cups
- Water – 3½ quarts
- Whole cloves - 12
- Cinnamon sticks - 4 (3 inches)
- Orange juice - 3/4 cup
- Lemon juice - 2/3 cup
- Sugar - 2 cups

Instructions

1. Add the cranberries, cloves, cinnamon, and water to your Dutch oven and bring to a boil.
2. Cover the pot, reduce the heat, and simmer for about 15 minutes.
3. Strain the cooked juice through cheese cloth or sieve. Squeeze gently.
4. Add the lemon juice, orange juice, and sugar to the strained juice.
5. Stir to dissolve the sugar completely.
6. Serve.

Nutrition Fact

Calories: 74 | Protein: 0g | Carbohydrates: 19g | Fiber: 1g | Sugar: 18g | Fat: 0g

Paprika Mixed Potato Mash

Total Time: 35 minutes; Prep Time: 20 minutes; Cook Time: 15 minutes
Servings: 12

Ingredients

- Medium yukon gold potatoes (peeled & cubed) - 6
- Medium sweet potatoes (peeled & cubed) - 2
- 2% milk - 1/2 cup
- Gouda cheese (shredded) - 1 cup
- Paprika - 1 teaspoon
- Salt - 1/2 teaspoon
- Pepper - 1/2 teaspoon

Instructions

1. Place the sweet potatoes and Yukon Gold to your Dutch oven and cover with water.
2. Bring mixture to a boil and lower the heat.
3. Without covering the pot, cook for about 15 minutes or until it becomes tender. Drain and return it to the pot.
4. Mash the potatoes while adding the milk gradually.
5. Stir in the paprika, cheese, pepper, and salt.
6. Serve.

Nutrition Fact
Calories: 178 | Protein: 6g | Carbohydrates: 33g | Fiber: 3g | Sugar: 6g | Fat: 3g

Jambalaya Rice

Servings: 4

Ingredients

- Hot link sausage (cut into ½" Pieces) - 1 lb
- Onions (chopped) - 2
- Parsley (chopped) - 1 cup
- Garlic (chopped) - 4 cloves
- Tomatoes - 1 (15-oz) can
- Thyme - 1 tsp
- Salt - 1/2 tsp
- Dry instant rice - 2 cups
- Water - 2 cups
- Shrimp (peeled, frozen) - 1 lb

Instructions

1. With some coals under, heat your Dutch oven.
2. Add the onions and sausage to the pot and cook for 5 minutes.
3. Stir in the parsley and garlic. Cook until the parsley becomes soft.
4. Add the tomatoes, salt, water, thyme, and rice. Bring the mixture to a boil.
5. Add the shrimp and stir.
6. Prepare a ring of 5 briquettes. Place the pot on it.
7. Cover the pot and place 10 briquettes on the lid.
8. Simmer for about 15 minutes, or until the rice becomes tender.
9. Serve.

Shrimp Jambalaya

Total Time: 40 minutes; Prep Time: 15 minutes; Cook Time: 25 minutes
Servings: 4

Ingredients

- Jambalaya mix - 1 package (8 ounces)
- Hot smoked sausage (slice into ½" Slices) - 1 package (14 ounces)
- Uncooked shrimp (peeled, deveined, chopped into ¾" Pieces) - 1 cup
- Green onions (thinly sliced) - 3
- Cheddar cheese (shredded) - 1/2 cup
- Pico de gallo - 1/2 cup

Instructions

1. Cook the jambalaya mix following the instructions on the package.
2. During the last 5 minutes of cooking, add the shrimp and sausage.
3. Remove it from the heat and stir in the green onions, pick de gallo, and cheese.
4. Cook to heat through.
5. Serve.

Nutrition Fact
Calories: 601 | Protein: 28g | Carbohydrates: 48g | Fiber: 1g | Sugar: 3g | Fat: 32g

Spaghetti Sauce Egg Lasagna

Servings: 18

Ingredients

- Lean ground beef - 2 pounds
- Minced garlic - 2 teaspoons
- Large onion (chopped) - 1
- Spaghetti sauce - 2 (26-ounce) jars
- Salt - 1/2 teaspoon
- Black pepper (ground) - 1/2 teaspoon
- Italian seasoning blend - 2 teaspoons
- Ricotta cheese - 2 (15-ounce) tubs
- Eggs - 2
- Lasagna noodles (uncooked) - 1 (16-ounce) box
- Mozzarella cheese - 1½ pounds (6 cups)

Instructions

1. Preheat your Dutch oven over 32 coals.
2. Add the beef, onion, and garlic. Cook until the beef turns brown. Remove the pot from heat.
3. Add the Italian seasoning, spaghetti sauce, black pepper, and salt to the pot and mix thoroughly.
4. Add the eggs and cheese to a bowl and mix. See it aside.
5. Line another Dutch oven with aluminum foil and spread 1/3 of the beef mixture in the pot.
6. Add 1/3 of the noodles on top, and then 1/3 of the egg mixture.

7. Then layer 1/3 of the mozzarella cheese.

8. Repeat the steps until the ingredients finish, about 2 more times.

9. With 11 coal briquettes under and 21 coals on the pot lid, bake until the noodles are fully cooked, about 45 minutes.

Leek Minestrone

Total Time: 45 minutes

Servings: 4

Ingredients

- Extra-virgin olive oil - 2 teaspoons
- Medium leeks (trimmed, washed, and thinly sliced) - 3
- Low-sodium chicken broth - 4 cups
- Water - 1 cup
- Large red potato (diced) - 1
- Dried thyme - 2 teaspoons
- Salt - ¼ teaspoon
- Freshly ground pepper - ½ teaspoon
- Whole-wheat orzo - ½ cup
- White beans (rinsed) - 1 (15 ounce) can
- Medium zucchini (quartered & thinly sliced) - 2
- Fresh spinach (stems removed) - 1 pound
- Cider vinegar - 2 tablespoons
- Freshly grated Parmesan cheese - 2 tablespoons

Instructions

1. Add the oil to your Dutch oven and heat over medium-high heat.
2. Add the leeks and cook for about 3 minutes. Stir occasionally.
3. Stir in the water, broth, pepper, thyme, potatoes, and salt. Bring the mixture to a boil.
4. Lower the heat to low, cover the pot, and simmer for about 5 minutes.

5. Stir in the orzo and cook for 5 minutes. Stir occasionally.
6. Add the zucchini and beans. Cook for about 8 minutes, or until the pasta becomes tender.
7. Add the spinach and cook for 2 minutes, or until it gets wilted.
8. Season with vinegar and transfer to your serving bowl.
9. Garnish with the Parmesan and serve.

Nutrition Fact

Calories: 299 | Protein: 18.2g | Carbohydrates: 54.5g | Fiber: 13.8g | Fat: 4.8g

Pumpkin Onion Chili

Total Time: 1 hour 15 minutes; Prep Time: 30 minutes; Cook
Time: 45 minutes

Servings: 8

Ingredients

- Extra-virgin olive oil - 1 tablespoon
- Chopped onion - 3 cups
- Carrot (chopped) - 1½ cups
- Large cloves garlic (minced) - 3
- Low-sodium vegetable broth - 4 cups
- Diced pumpkin - 3 cups
- Crushed tomatoes (no-salt-added) - 1 (28 ounce) can
- Low-sodium beans (rinsed) - 4 (15 ounce) cans
- Chili powder - 3 tablespoons
- Ground cumin - 2 teaspoons
- Ground cinnamon - 1 teaspoon
- Salt - ¾ teaspoon
- Cayenne pepper - ¼ teaspoon
- For garnish, use diced onion, pepitas, sliced jalapeños, and/or cotija cheese

Instructions

1. Add the oil to your Dutch oven and heat over medium-high heat.
2. Add the onion cook for about 5 minutes until it starts to turn brown. Stir often.

3. Lower the heat to medium.
4. Add the carrot and cook for about 5 minutes.
5. Stir in the garlic and cook for 1 minute. Stir constantly.
6. Stir in the broth and scrape the brown bits from the bottom of the pot. Bring mixture to a boil over high heat.
7. Add the pumpkin, beans, cumin, tomatoes, cinnamon, cayenne, chili powder, and salt.
8. Cover the pot and return to a boil. Lower the heat to gentle summer.
9. Cook for about 30 minutes, until the pumpkin becomes tender.
10. Garnish with onion, cheese, jalapenos, and pepitas.
11. Serve.

Nutrition Fact

Calories: 276 | Protein: 13.9g | Carbohydrates: 49g | Fiber: 16.5g | Fat: 2.8g

Zucchini Ratatouille

Servings: 4

Ingredients

- Large globe eggplant (peeled, coarsely chopped) - 1
- Large zucchini (sliced into ¼" Thick rounds) - 1
- Kosher salt - 2 teaspoons (plus extra)
- Olive oil (divided) - ¾ cup
- Thyme - 5 sprigs
- Large onion (halved, sliced ½" Thick) - 1
- Red bell pepper (ribs & seeds removed, coarsely chopped) - 1
- Garlic (thinly sliced) – 2 cloves
- Cherry tomatoes (divided) - 2 pints
- Black pepper (freshly ground)
- Torn basil leaves - 1 cup

Instructions

1. Preheat your oven to 400F.
2. Put the zucchini, eggplant, and 2 teaspoons of salt in a colander and toss.
3. Allow the mixture to sit for 30 minutes. Par dry it with paper towels.
4. Add ¼ cup of oil to your Dutch oven and heat over medium-high heat.
5. Add half of the zucchini mixture to the pot and cook for about 5 minutes, or until the vegetables start to change color. Stir constantly. Transfer it to a bowl.
6. Cook the remaining with ¼ cup of oil.
7. Tie the thyme sprigs with twine.

8. Add the remaining oil to the pot and heat.

9. Stir in the garlic, onion, thyme, and bell pepper. Cook for about 10 minutes or until the onion becomes soft. Stir occasionally.

10. Add half of the tomatoes and cook for about 5 minutes. Stir occasionally.

11. Add the eggplant and zucchini and stir.

12. Add the remaining tomatoes and season with pepper and salt.

13. Transfer the pot to the oven and roast for about 20 minutes, until the vegetables become soft.

14. Remove the thyme bundles.

15. Transfer to your serving plate and top with the basil.

Tomato Meatball Pasta

Servings: 8

Ingredients
- Mild Italian sausage (uncooked, removed casings) - 1 pound
- Unsalted butter (divided) - 3 tablespoons
- Finely chopped onion - 1/2 cup
- Kosher salt - 1 teaspoon
- Black pepper (freshly ground) - 1/4 teaspoon
- Garlic (minced) - 1 clove
- Tomato paste - 1 tablespoon
- Crushed tomatoes - 1 (28-ounce) can
- Water (you can use low-sodium chicken broth) – 2-3 cups
- Apple cider vinegar - 1 tablespoon
- Granulated sugar - 2 teaspoons
- Dried oregano - 1 teaspoon
- Dry o-shaped pasta - 8 ounces (2 cups)
- For serving, use red pepper flakes and Parmesan cheese

Instructions
1. Divide sausage into 32 equal portions (about ½ ounce each). Roll them into meatballs.
2. Add 2 tablespoons of butter to your Dutch oven and melt over medium-high heat.
3. Add the meatballs and cook each side for about 3 minutes, or until they turn brown. Turn occasionally.
4. Transfer the meatballs to a plate.

5. Add the remaining butter to the pot and heat over medium-high heat.
6. Add the onion, pepper, and salt. Scrape the brown bits at the bottom of the pot and cook for about 5 minutes.
7. Stir in the tomato paste and garlic. Cook for a minute.
8. Add vinegar, tomatoes, sugar, 2 cups of water, and oregano.
9. Stir in the meatballs and pasta. Bring the mixture to a boil.
10. Lower the heat to medium-low and simmer for about 30 minutes, or until the pasta is well cooked. Stir occasionally. You can add more water/broth.
11. Transfer to serving bowl and top with the red pepper flakes and Parmesan cheese.
12. Serve.

Nutrition Fact

Calories: 394 | Protein: 15.2g | Carbohydrates: 32.3g | Fiber: 3.1g | Sugar: 7g | Fat: 23.3g

Leek And Squash Lasagna

Total Time: 2 hour 45 minutes

Servings: 1

Ingredients

- Lasagna noodles - 10 ounces
- Unsalted butter - 2 tablespoons
- Leeks (white and pale green parts only, sliced, and washed) - 4 large (~ 6 cups)
- All-purpose flour - ½ cup
- Nonfat milk - 4 cups
- Dried thyme - 1 teaspoon
- Salt - 1 teaspoon
- Freshly grated nutmeg - ¾ teaspoon
- Freshly ground pepper - ½ teaspoon
- Butternut squash (peeled, cut into halves, seeded and grated) - 2 pound
- Parmigiano-reggiano (grated) - 6 ounces
- Toasted pine nuts - 1/4 cup

Instructions

1. Preheat your oven to 350F.
2. Coat your baking dish (9x13") with cooking spray.
3. Add enough water to your lot and bring to a boil.
4. Cook the noodles for about 2 minutes. Drain and return to the pot. Cover with water.
5. Add the butter to your Dutch oven and heat over medium heat.

6. Add the leeks and cook for about 6 minutes. Stir often.
7. Add the flour and stir constantly. Cook for 2 minutes.
8. Stir in the milk and cook for about 10 minutes, or until it becomes thick and starts to bubble. Stir constantly.
9. Stir in the nutmeg, thyme, salt, and pepper.
10. Remove the pot from heat.
11. Assemble the lasagna by layering 1/3 of the noodles, 1/3 of the sauce, 1/3 of the cheese, and ½ of the squash. Divide the remaining into 2 and layer on top with the pine nuts.
12. Use parchment paper to cover it. The cover with foil.
13. Bake for about 50 minutes.
14. Uncover and bake for extra 45 minutes, or until it slightly turns brown.
15. Allow it to stand for about 10 minutes before serving.

Nutrition Fact
Calories: 275 | Protein: 12.6g | Carbohydrates: 38.2g | Fiber: 6.6g | Fat: 8.8g

Elbow Mac & Cheese

Total Time: 32 minutes; Prep Time: 10 minutes; Cook Time: 22 minutes
Servings: 8

Ingredients

- Whole milk - 2 cups
- Water - 1 3/4 cups
- Kosher salt - 1 teaspoon
- Dry elbow macaroni - 1 pound
- Sharp cheddar cheese (shredded) - 8 ounces (~ 2 cups)
- Unsalted butter - 2 tablespoons
- Black pepper (freshly ground)

Instructions

1. Add the milk, salt, and water in your Dutch oven. Bring mixture to a boil over medium-high heat.
2. Lower the heat to medium and stir in the macaroni.
3. Simmer for about 10 minutes, or until the pasta becomes tender.
4. Meanwhile, shred the cheddar cheese.
5. Remove the pot from heat.
6. Stir in the butter, and cheese. Stir until the butter melts completely.
7. Too with the black pepper and serve.

Garlic Rice Shrimp Casserole

Servings: 6

Ingredients

- Vegetable oil - 2 tablespoons
- Medium yellow onion (diced) - 1
- Long-grain white rice - 1 1/2 cups
- Garlic (finely chopped, divided) - 3 cloves
- Fresh ginger (finely chopped, peeled) - 1 teaspoon
- Kosher salt - 1 teaspoon
- Red pepper flakes - 1/4 teaspoon (optional)
- Low-sodium chicken broth - 2 cups
- Water (divided) - 3/4 cup (+ 1 tablespoon)
- Frozen broccoli florets - 12 ounces
- Frozen shrimp (peeled, uncooked, deveined) - 12 ounces
- Honey - 1/4 cup
- Tamari (you can use soy sauce) - 2 tablespoons
- Cornstarch - 1 teaspoon

Instructions

1. Add the oil to your Dutch oven and heat over medium heat.
2. Add the onion and cook for about 10 minutes. Stir occasionally.
3. Add the rice, ginger, red pepper flakes, 2 cloves of garlic, and salt.
4. Cook for 3 minutes, stir occasionally.
5. Add ¾ cup of water and broth to the pot. Bring mixture to a boil.
6. Lower the heat to medium-low, cover the pot, and simmer for 10 minutes.

7. Stir in the shrimp and broccoli, cover the pot, and simmer for 30 minutes, or until the shrimp cooks through.
8. Add the tamari, honey, and the remaining garlic in a saucepan and bring to a simmer over medium heat.
9. Add the remaining water and cornstarch to a bowl and stir to dissolve the cornstarch.
10. Transfer the mixture to the simmering sauce and continue to stir for about 30 seconds until it becomes thick.
11. Remove the pot from heat.
12. Drizzle the sauce over the rice and serve.

Nutrition Fact

Calories: 343 | Protein: 15g | Carbohydrates: 57.7g | Fiber: 0.4g | Sugar: 12.5g | Fat: 6.3g

Tomato Braised Rabbit

Total Time: 1 hour 45 minutes; Prep Time: 15 minutes; Cook Time: 1 hour 30 minutes

Servings: 4

Ingredients

- Rabbit (dressed, cut into serving-size pieces) – 1 (~ 2 1/2 pounds)
- Salt to taste
- Black pepper (fresh ground)
- Olive oil - 1/4 cup
- Onion (diced) - 1
- Celery ribs (diced) - 2
- Garlic (chopped) - 4 cloves
- Salt - 1 teaspoon
- Balsamic vinegar - 1 tablespoon
- White wine - 1/2 cup
- Tomato (chopped) - 1 cup
- Chicken stock (or broth) - 2 cups
- Rosemary (dried) - 1 teaspoon
- Thyme (dried) - 1 teaspoon
- Oregano (dried) - 1/2 teaspoon

Instructions

1. Preheat your oven to 350F.
2. Season the rabbit meat with black pepper and salt.
3. Add the oil to your Dutch oven and heat over medium-high heat.

4. Add the rabbit and cook to brown all sides.

5. Transfer the meat to a plate and set it aside.

6. Add the onions, garlic, celery, and 1 teaspoon of salt to the pot.

7. Lower the heat to medium and saute for about 3 minutes.

8. Add the wine and vinegar. Stir to scrape the brown bits off the bottom of the pot.

9. Bring the mixture to a boil and cook for 2 minutes.

10. Stir in the tomatoes, rosemary, chicken stock, oregano, and thyme.

11. Return the rabbit pieces to the pot and stir very well to combine.

12. Transfer to the oven and cook for 1 hour 30 minutes, or until the rabbit is tender.

13. Remove from heat and stir in the parsley.

14. Allow it to rest for about 20 minutes.

15. Serve.

Nutrition Fact

Calories: 783 | Protein: 92g | Carbohydrates: 20g | Fat: 33g

Pasta With Basil And White Beans

Total Time: 20 minutes; Prep Time: 10 minutes; Cook Time: 10 minutes
Servings: 4

Ingredients

- Water - 4 cups
- Salt (divided) - 1½ tsp.
- Small shell (or bow tie) pasta - 1½ cups
- Great northern beans - 2 cans
- Olive oil - 3 tbsp.
- Onion (diced) - 1
- Garlic (minced) - 3 cloves
- Fresh basil (chopped) - 2 tsp.
- Dried oregano - 1 tsp.
- Pepper - 1/2 tsp.
- Paprika - 1½ tbsp.
- Tomato sauce - 1 cup

Instructions

1. Add the pasta to water with 1 tsp of water and cook.
2. Drain and reserve about 1/3 cup of the cooking liquid.
3. Add the beans. Cover it and set aside.
4. Add the oil to your Dutch oven and heat.
5. Add the onion, basil, oregano, garlic, pepper, and the remaining salt.
6. Saute for about 5 minutes, or until the onions become soft.
7. Transfer the mixture to the beans mixture and heat over low heat.

8. Add the tomato sauce and paprika, and stir thoroughly to blend well.
9. Serve.

Nutrition Fact

Calories: 521 | Protein: 21g | Carbohydrates: 85g | Fat: 12g

Potato Sausage

Total Time: 35 minutes; Prep Time: 10 minutes; Cook Time: 25 minutes
Servings: 8

Ingredients

- Sausage - 2 pounds
- Frozen hash brown potatoes - 2 pounds
- Eggs (beaten with ¼ cup of water) - 8
- Cheese (grated) - 2 cups

Instructions

1. Place your dutch oven over bed of 8 hot coals. Add the sausage to the pot. Cook and crumble.
2. Remove the sausage from pot and drain it with paper towels.
3. Add the potatoes to the pot and cook until they turn brown.
4. Spread the potatoes and place the sausage over it.
5. Spread the egg on the sausage and sprinkle with the cheese.
6. With the 8 coals under, cover the pot and place 16 coals on the pot lid.
7. Cook for about 25 minutes.
8. Serve.

Vegetarian Celery Chili

Total Time: 60 minutes; Prep Time: 20 minutes; Cook Time: 40 minutes
Servings: 8

Ingredients

- Olive oil - 2 tablespoons
- Large yellow onion (diced) - 1
- Large bell peppers (diced) - 2
- Medium carrots (diced) - 2
- Celery (diced) - 2 stalks
- Garlic (minced) - 4 cloves
- Chili powder - 2 tablespoons
- Ground cumin - 1 tablespoon
- Dried oregano - 2 teaspoons
- Kosher salt - 2 teaspoons (plus extra)
- Freshly ground black pepper - 1/2 teaspoon
- Cayenne pepper - 1/4 teaspoon
- Diced tomatoes (fire-roasted, not drained) - 1 (28-ounce) can
- Roasted green chiles (not drained) - 2 (4-ounce) cans
- Beans (drained & rinsed) - 3 (15-ounce) cans
- Low-sodium vegetable broth (divided) – 1-2 cups
- Whole kernel corn (drained) - 1 (15-ounce) can
- Serving suggestions: Lime wedges, sliced avocado, shredded cheddar cheese, sliced jalapeño, cilantro leaves with tender stems, toasted pumpkin seeds, pickled red onion, sliced radishes

Instructions

1. Add the oil to your Dutch oven and heat over medium heat.
2. Add the bell peppers, onion, celery, carrot, and garlic. Cook for about 10 minutes, or until it becomes tender. Stir constantly.
3. Add the cumin, salt, chili powder, oregano, cayenne, and black pepper. Toss to coat well.
4. Stir in the chiles, tomatoes, 1 cup of broth, and beans. Stir very well to combine.
5. Bring mixture to a boil and lower the heat.
6. Simmer for about 40 minutes until the chicken becomes thick. You can add more broth if you desire.
7. Stir in the corn and mix to combine.
8. Transfer to your serving bowls with toppings of choice.
9. Serve.

Nutrition Fact

Calories: 207 | Protein: 9g | Carbohydrates: 31.6g | Fiber: 6.4g | Sugar: 5.4g | Fat: 6.4g

Almond Peach Crisp

Total Time: 65 minutes; Prep Time: 20 minutes; Cook Time: 45 minutes
Servings: 8

Ingredients

- Large peaches (peeled, seeds removed, and cit into slices) - 7 (~ 3 pounds)
- Lemon juice - 2 tbs
- Granulated sugar - 1/2 cup
- Lemon zest - 1 lemon
- Cornstarch - 2 tbs
- Old-fashion oatmeal - 1 cup
- All-purpose flour - 1/2 cup
- Almond slices - 1/2 cup
- Light brown sugar (packed) - 1/2 cup
- Ground cinnamon - 1/2 tsp
- Ground ginger - 1/2 tsp
- Salt - 1/8 tsp
- Cold unsalted butter (cut into small pieces) - 1/3 cup

Instructions

1. Prepare 22 coal briquettes.
2. Add the peaches, sugar, lemon zest and juice, and cornstarch to a bowl and mix to combine. Set it aside.
3. Add other ingredients together in a separate bowl.

4. Add the butter to the dry mixture and rub with your finger to form coarse crumbs.
5. Add the peach mixture to your Dutch oven.
6. Sprinkle the topping mixture on top and cover the pot.
7. Make a bed of 8 coals and place the pot on it.
8. Place the remaining coal on the pot lid.
9. Bake until the topping turns golden brown, about 45 minutes.
10. Remove from heat and allow it to cool down for about 10 minutes.
11. Serve.

Nutrition Fact

Calories: 268 | Protein: 4g | Carbohydrates: 45g | Fiber: 4g | Sugar: 33g | Fat: 10g

Salmon Mashed Potato Cauliflower

Total Time: 30 minutes

Servings: 6

Ingredients

- Canola oil - 1 tablespoon
- Chopped carrot - ⅓ cup
- Chopped celery - ⅓ cup
- Reduced-sodium chicken broth - 4 cups
- Water - 1 ½ cups
- Skinned salmon fillet - 1 (12 ounce)
- Cauliflower florets (chopped) - 2 ½ cups
- Chopped fresh chives - 3 tablespoons
- Instant mashed potato flakes - 1 ⅓ cups
- Chopped fresh dill - 1/4 cup
- Dijon mustard - 1 tablespoon
- Salt - ¼ teaspoon
- Freshly ground pepper - to taste

Instructions

1. Add the oil to your Dutch oven and heat over medium heat.
2. Add the celery and carrot. Cook for about 4 minutes, or until the vegetables turn brown. Stir frequently.
3. Add the water, broth, salmon, chives, and cauliflower. Bring the mixture to a simmer.
4. Cover the pot and cook until the salmon cooks through, about 8 minutes.

5. Transfer the salmon to your cutting board and shred it into bite-sizes.
6. Stir in the dill, flakes, and mustard into the soup until it becomes well blended.
7. Set to simmer and add the salmon back into the pot.
8. Rehear, and season with pepper and salt.

Nutrition Fact

Calories: 178 | Protein: 17.1g | Carbohydrates: 16.9g | Fiber: 2.3g | Fat: 5.6g

Chapter 3

BEEF AND PORK

Tomato Black Bean Beef

Total Time: 45 minutes; Prep Time: 20 minutes; Cook Time: 25 minutes
Servings: 8

Ingredients

- 95% lean ground beef - 1 ½ pounds
- Sliced celery, coarsely chopped carrots, chopped sweet peppers and/or chopped onions - 3 cups
- Garlic (minced) - 4 cloves
- Canola oil - 1 tablespoon
- Black beans (no-salt-added, rinsed, and drained) - 2 (15 ounce) cans
- Diced tomatoes (no-salt-added, not drained) - 2 (14.5 ounce) cans
- Tomato sauce - 1 (15 ounce) can
- Low-sodium beef broth - 1 cup
- Chili powder - 2 tablespoons
- Dried oregano (crushed) - 1 teaspoon
- Black pepper - ½ teaspoon
- Chopped onion, sliced green onion, snipped fresh parsley, chopped tomato, snipped fresh cilantro, and/or plain fat-free greek yogurt
- Chili powder - 1

Instructions

1. Add the beef, garlic, and vegetables to your Dutch oven and cook over medium-high heat until the beef turns brown. Break the meat into crumbles and drain.

2. Add the canned tomatoes, beans, broth, oregano, tomato sauce, black pepper, and chili powder. Stir mixture and bring to a boil.

3. Lower the heat, cover the pot, and simmer for 20 minutes. Stir occasionally.

4. Transfer to your serving bowl.

5. Serve with onion, green onion, cilantro, fresh tomatoes, parsley and yogurt, sprinkled with chili powder.

Nutrition Fact

Calories: 267 | Protein: 26.2g | Carbohydrates: 26.8g | Fiber: 8.7g | Fat: 6.4g

Thick-Cut Pork Chops

Total Time: 40 minutes; Prep Time: 28 minutes; Cook Time: 12 minutes
Servings: 2

Ingredients

- Thick-cut pork chops (1 - 1.5-inch thick, bone-in,) - 4
- Olive oil - 2 tablespoons
- Kosher salt - 1 teaspoon
- Black pepper (freshly cracked) - 1/2 teaspoon
- Garlic powder - 1/2 teaspoon
- For serving, use lemon wedges (optional)

Instructions

1. Add ¼ cup of kosher salt to 1 quart of warm water and stir until the salt is absorbed.
2. Add the pork chops in the water and brine for about 15 minutes. You can as well cover and refrigerate for 6 hours.
3. Remove the pork chop and rinse with cold water. Pat dry with paper towels.
4. Preheat your oven to 375F.
5. Brush both sides if the pork chops with olive oil.
6. Add the pepper, garlic powder, and salt in a separate bowl and whisk together until the mixture is well combined.
7. Sprinkle both sides of the pork chops with the mixture.
8. Meanwhile, heat your skillet (cast iron) over high heat on a stove-top for about 5 minutes.

9. Once the skillet is hot, add the pork chops and evenly press them into the pan. This will help all the bottom surface of the pork chops to have contact with the pan

10. Cook for about 3 minutes. Flip and make for another 3 minutes.

11. Flip once more, and bake for about 3-5 minutes, or until the internal temperature gets to 145F.

12. Transfer the pork to your serving plate with the juice. Allow it to rest for 3 minutes or more.

13. Serve. You can store it up to 3 days in your refrigerator with airtight container.

Mushroom Beef Goulash

Servings: 8

Ingredients

- Beef tips (cut into 2" Cubes) - 2 lb
- Paprika - 2 tsp
- Small onion - 1
- Salt – 1½ tsp
- Vegetable oil - 3 tbsp
- Pepper - 1/4 tsp
- Diced tomatoes (not drained) - 1 can
- Sour cream - 1 cup
- Whole mushrooms - 4 oz
- Flour - 2 tbsp

Instructions

1. Preheat your oven to 325F.
2. Add the oil and heat.
3. Add the beef tips and onion. Cook until it turns brown.
4. Stir in the mushrooms, tomatoes, and seasonings.
5. Cover the pot and simmer for about 1 hour 30 minutes, or until the meat becomes tender.
6. Mix the sour cream and flour in a bowl.
7. Add the mixture to the pot and stir well.
8. Cook to heat through.
9. Serve over spaghetti or noodles.

Beef Tacos

Total Time: 3 hours; Prep Time: 30 minutes; Cook Time: 2 hours 30 minutes

Servings: 6

Ingredients

- Canola oil - 2 tablespoons
- Beef short ribs (bone-in) - 6
- Salt - 1/4 teaspoon
- Pepper - 1/4 teaspoon
- Medium carrots (finely chopped) - 2
- Small yellow onion (finely chopped) - 1
- Baking cocoa - 2 tablespoons
- Tomato sauce - 1 can (15 ounces)
- Beef broth - 1 bottle (12 ounces)
- Water (optional)
- Corn tortillas (warmed) – 12 (6 inches)
- Pico de gallo - 3/4 cup
- Queso fresco (or use crumbled feta cheese) - 3/4 cup

Instructions

1. Preheat your oven to 325F.
2. Add the oil to your Dutch oven and heat over medium-high heat.
3. Sprinkle the beef with pepper and salt, and cook until it turns brown. Remove it from the pot.
4. Lower the heat to medium.

5. Add the onion and carrots to the pot and cook in the drippings for about 5 minutes, or until it starts to turn brown. Stir frequently.

6. Add the cocoa and toast for 2 minutes. Stir frequently.

7. Stir in the broth and tomato sauce.

8. Scrape brown bits from the bottom of the Dutch oven and bring to a boil.

9. Simmer for extra 3 minutes.

10. Return the ribs back to the pot. You can add water if it's too thick.

11. Cover and bake for about 2-3 hours.

12. Remove from heat and drain it. Reserve the juice and allow it to cool.

13. Remove the ribs from the pot. Remove bones from the ribs and discard the bones.

14. Shred the meat with your forks. Skim fat from the juice.

15. Return the juice and meat to the pot, and heat through.

16. Serve on the corn tortillas with queso fresco and pico de gallo.

Nutrition Fact

Calories: 508 | Protein: 37g | Carbohydrates: 32g | Fiber: 6g | Sugar: 4g | Fat: 26g

Stewed Tomato Beef Chili

Total Time: 1 hour 50 minutes; Prep Time: 20 minutes; Cook Time: 1 hour 30 minutes

Servings: 1

Ingredients

- Canola oil - 2 tablespoons
- Ground beef (90% lean) - 4 pounds
- Medium onions (chopped) - 2
- Medium green pepper (chopped) - 1
- Kidney beans (rinsed & drained) - 4 cans (16 ounces each)
- Stewed tomatoes (cut up) - 3 cans (28 ounces each)
- Beef broth - 1 can (14-1/2 ounces)
- Chili powder - 3 tablespoons
- Ground coriander - 2 tablespoons
- Ground cumin - 2 tablespoons
- Garlic (minced) - 4
- Dried oregano - 1 teaspoon

Instructions

1. Add the oil to your Dutch oven and heat over medium heat.
2. Add the beef and cook until it turns brown, crumbling. Drain the meat and set it aside.
3. Add the green pepper and onions, and cook until it becomes tender.
4. Return the meat to the Dutch oven.
5. Add other ingredients, stir, and bring to a boil.
6. Lower the heat, cover, simmer for about 1 hour 30 minutes.

7. Serve.

Nutrition Fact

Calories: 354 | Protein: 31g | Carbohydrates: 32g | Fiber: 8g | Sugar: 10g | Fat: 12g

Beef Potato Pot Roast

Servings: 8

Ingredients

- Rump roast (you can use pot roast) - 3 lb
- Vegetable oil - 3 tbsp
- Potatoes (peeled, sliced) - 4
- Carrots (peeled, sliced) - 4
- Onions (peeled, sliced) - 2
- Salt - 1 tsp
- Pepper - 1/4 tsp
- Water - 1/2 cup

Instructions

1. Add the oil to your Dutch oven and heat to 350F.
2. Add the roast and brown on all sides.
3. Season with pepper and salt.
4. Add the veggies and water.
5. Cover the pot and bake at 300F for about 3 hours.

Coconut Milk And Chicken With Lemongrass

Servings: 6

Ingredients

- Whole roasting chicken - 1 (3 - 4 pounds)
- Sea salt
- Black pepper (freshly ground)
- Butter - 4 tablespoons
- Olive oil - 1 tablespoon
- Cinnamon stick - 1
- Whole star anise - 2
- Cilantro stems (roughly chopped) - 1/2 cup
- Large lemon (cut into eighths) - 1
- Lemongrass (use only 5 inches of white part, cut into ¼" Pieces) - 1 stalk
- Garlic (peeled and smashed) - 6 - 8 cloves
- Coconut milk - 1 (14 - 16-ounce) can
- Torn greens - 3 cups
- Green onions (cut into ¼" Pieces) - 2
- Cilantro (chopped) to garnish
- Cooked rice (to serve)

Instructions

1. Pat dry the chicken and season with pepper and salt. Cover and set aside.
2. Preheat your oven to 375F.

3. Add the butter to your Dutch oven and melt over medium heat. Add the oil and heat.
4. With the breast side facing up, place the chicken in the pot and sizzle for about 30 seconds.
5. Gently flip and cook for another 30 seconds.
6. Remove the out from hear and transfer the chicken to a plate. Discard the fat from the pot.
7. Return the chicken back into the pot, with the breast side facing up.
8. Stir in the star anise, cinnamon stick, lemon, cilantro, coconut milk, garlic, and lemongrass.
9. Cook for about 85 minutes, scooping the sauce on the chicken every 20 minutes.
10. Once done, transfer the chicken to a plate.
11. Discard the star anise and cinnamon stick.
12. Return the pot to the heat (medium heat) and stir in the spinach for about 10 seconds.
13. Carve chicken and place on the rice.
14. Spoon the sauce over and garnish with cilantro leaves, and scallions.

Nutrition Fact

Calories: 662 | Protein: 35.6g | Carbohydrates: 7.8g | Fiber: 1.5g | Sugar: 0.7g | Fat: 55.2g

Oven Roasted Dry Rub Pulled Pork

Total Time: 12 hours 20 minutes; Prep Time: 20 minutes; Cook Time: 12 hours

Servings: 8

Ingredients

- Pork shoulder roast – 4 pound
- Liquid smoke - 1 teaspoon (optional)

For the Dry Rub

- Brown sugar - 2 tablespoon
- Salt - 1 tablespoon
- Black pepper (freshly ground) - 1 tablespoon
- Paprika - 1 tablespoon
- Chili powder - 2 teaspoon
- Garlic powder - 2 teaspoon
- Onion powder - 2 teaspoon
- Ground cumin - 2 teaspoon
- Cayenne - 1 teaspoon

Instructions

1. Pat dry the meat with paper towels and trim off excess fat.
2. Add the rub ingredients in a bowl and mix thoroughly.
3. Toss the pork to coat completely.
4. Preheat your oven to 215F.
5. Place the pork neat in your Dutch oven.
6. Add 1/3 cup of water in a ramekin. Add the liquid smoke to it.

7. Place the ramekin in the Dutch oven.

8. Cover the pot and place it in the middle of the oven.

9. Roast for about 12 hours or until the pork is tender.

10. Allow to rest for about 1 hour.

11. Transfer the pork to a cutting board and pull apart into smaller pieces with your forks.

12. Taste and adjust seasonings as desired.

13. Serve on soft rolls, splashed with BBQ sauce.

Soy Braised Short Ribs

Total Time: 2 hours 20 minutes; Prep Time: 20 minutes; Cook Time: 2 hours

Servings: 4

Ingredients

- Sugar - 5 tbsp
- Soy sauce - 6 tbsp
- Mirin (japanese rice wine) - 2 tbsp
- Garlic (finely chopped) - 4 cloves
- Onion (grated) - 1/2
- Scallions (finely chopped) - 3
- Sesame seeds - 1 tbsp
- Sesame oil - 1 tbsp
- Asian pear (peeled & finely chopped) - 1/2
- Thick-cut short ribs (rinsed in cold water) - 3 lbs
- Small potatoes (chopped into large chunks) - 2
- Medium carrots (chopped into 2" Lengths) – 2

Instructions

1. Score the ribs to absorb more braising liquid.
2. Add all the ingredients for marinade in a bowl and mix.
3. Put the ribs in your Dutch oven and pour the braising liquid inside. Stir to cover the ribs and heat over high heat.
4. Cover the pot and bring to a boil.

5. Lower the heat to a gentle simmer, and cook for about 90 minutes or more. Add the carrots and potatoes 30 minutes before the time.
6. Serve.

Pork Red Wine Ragu

Total Time: 3 hours 15 minutes; Prep Time: 15 minutes; Cook Time: 3 hours

Servings: 8

Ingredients

- Pork shoulder - 2 pounds
- Salt
- Pepper (freshly ground)
- Olive oil - 2 tablespoons
- Yellow onion (finely chopped) - 1
- Medium carrots (diced) - 2
- Celery rib (diced) - 1
- Garlic (minced) – 1 clove
- Tomato paste - 2 tablespoons
- Red wine - 1 cup
- Whole peeled tomatoes (chopped) - 1 (28-ounce) can
- Fresh thyme (stems discarded, leaves removed and chopped) - 6 sprigs
- Fresh rosemary - 1 (4-inch) sprig
- Pappardelle - 1 pound
- To serve use Parmesan cheese (freshly grated)

Instructions

1. Place rack in the middle of your oven and preheat the oven to 325F.
2. Season the pork with pepper, and salt.

3. Add 1 tablespoon of oil to your Dutch oven and heat over medium-high heat.
4. Add the pork and cook for about 15 minutes. Turn while cooking. Transfer it to a plate.
5. Add the remaining oil to the pot and heat over medium-high heat.
6. Stir in the onion, celery, garlic, and carrot. Scrape the brown bits from the bottom of the pot.
7. Cook for about 4 minutes.
8. Stir in the wine and tomato paste. Bring to a boil.
9. Cook for about 4 minutes, or until the wine reduces by half.
10. Add the tomatoes, rosemary, and thyme. Season with pepper and salt.
11. Return the pork to the pot.
12. Cover and bake for about 3 hours.
13. Discard the rosemary and shred the pork with 2 forks. Stir to combine
14. Serve over hot pasta, topped with Parmesan cheese.

Tender Braised Steak

Total Time: 2 hours; Prep Time: 30 minutes; Cook Time: 1 hour 30 minutes
Servings: 6

Ingredients

- Beef round steaks - 2 pounds (~ 6 steaks)
- Cooking oil - 2 ounces
- Large onion (peeled, cut into halves, and sliced) - 1
- All-purpose flour - 2 ounces
- Beef stock - 1½ cups
- Diced tomatoes (plus the liquid) - 1 (14.5 ounces) can
- Bay leaf - 1
- Kosher salt - 3 teaspoons
- Black pepper (freshly ground) - 1½ teaspoons

Instructions

1. Preheat your oven to 300F.
2. Pat dry the meat with paper towels.
3. Add the oil to your Dutch oven and heat.
4. Add the steaks and cook each side for about 4 minutes, or until it turns brown. Do this in batches to avoid overcrowding. Set them aside.
5. Add the onion and cook until it becomes translucent.
6. Add the flour and stir until it forms thick roux. Cook for a few minutes to brown it.
7. Stir in the stock and tomatoes.
8. Add black pepper and salt.

9. Stir in the bay leaf and simmer until the sauce starts to thicken, about 5 minutes.

10. Add the steaks to the sauce and submerge.

11. Cover the Dutch oven and transfer to the preheated oven.

12. Braise until the meat becomes tender, about 1 hour 30 minutes.

13. Serve.

Nutrition Fact

Calories: 414 | Protein: 44g | Carbohydrates: 12g | Fat: 21g

Pork Sausage Casserole

Servings: 8

Ingredients

- Butter - 1/4 cube
- Bread - 8 slices
- Precooked pork sausage - 2 lb
- Cheddar cheese (grated) - 1 lb
- Eggs - 12
- Milk - 1 qt
- Dry mustard - 1-1/2 tsp
- Salt - 1 tsp

Instructions

1. Spread the butter inside your Dutch oven.
2. Cut the bread into pieces.
3. Break the sausage into pieces.
4. Add the milk, salt, eggs, and dry mustard in a bowl and beat.
5. Layer bread, egg mixture, and sausage in the pot. Cover the pot.
6. Bake at 350F for about 25 minutes.
7. Pour in the cheese and bake for additional 15 minutes.

Oven-Braised Beer Corned Beef

Total Time: 5 hours 10 minutes; Prep Time: 10 minutes; Cook Time: 5 hours

Servings: 10

Ingredients

- Corned beef brisket - 1 (4 pound)
- Large onion (halved and sliced) - 1
- Black peppercorns - 1 teaspoon
- Whole allspice - 1/2 teaspoon
- Bay leaves - 2
- Beer - 2 cups
- Beef broth - 4 cups

Instructions

1. Under cold running water, rinse the beef brisket.
2. Add half of the onion to your Dutch oven.
3. Place the rinsed beef brisket on top and top with the remaining onion.
4. Sprinkle with the allspice and peppercorns.
5. Add the bay leaves
6. Heat your oven to 275F.
7. Add the beef broth and beer to a day and bring mixture to a boil.
8. Pour the broth mixture on the beef brisket.
9. Cover the pot and place in the oven.
10. Cook until the meat becomes tender, about 4 hours and more.
11. Slice the meat and transfer it to your serving bowl.

12. Add vegetables and drizzle with the braising liquid.

13. Serve.

Nutrition Fact

Calories: 482 | Protein: 56g | Carbohydrates: 4g | Fat: 24g

Stuffed Pork Chops With Cornstarch Glaze

Total Time: 1 hour 15 minutes; Prep Time: 15 minutes; Cook Time: 1 hour
Servings: 10

Ingredients

Stuffed Pork Chops

- Butter - ½ cup
- Celery (diced) - ½ cup
- Onion (diced) - ¾ cup
- Fresh bread cubes - 1 cup
- Parsley - 1 tablespoon
- Salt - 1 teaspoon
- Fresh pepper (ground) - 1 teaspoon
- Paprika - ½ teaspoon
- Rosemary - ½ teaspoon
- Allspice - ½ teaspoon
- Apple (peeled & diced) - 1
- Pork chops pocket - 10 (8 ounce)
- Olive oil - 2 ounces
- Water - ¾ cup

Glaze

- Sugar - 1pick
- Cornstarch - 2 tablespoons
- Oranges (zest & juice) - 2
- Cinnamon - 1 teaspoon
- Whole cloves - 14

- Salt - ½ teaspoon
- Extra orange slices for garnish

Instructions
1. Add the butter to your Dutch oven and melt over medium heat.
2. Add the onion, and celery. Saute until it becomes tender.
3. Add other ingredients. You can add small water if desired.
4. Stuff the pork chop pockets with the mixture.
5. Use toothpick to close them and tie them together with string.
6. Add the olive oil to the Dutch oven and heat it up.
7. Add the chops and brown both sides.
8. Poor the water and cover the pot.
9. Simmer for about 55 minutes at 350F.
10. Meanwhile, add the cornstarch and sugar to a separate Dutch oven.
11. Add the orange juice and zest, cloves, cinnamon, and salt.
12. Cook the sauce over medium heat, or until it becomes thick.
13. Pour the sauce over the pork chops and serve.

Green Chile Pork Verde

Total Time: 65 minutes; Prep Time: 15 minutes; Cook Time: 50 minutes
Servings: 18

Ingredients

- Lean pork (chopped into small cubes) - 5 pounds
- Chopped onion- 1
- Celery (finely chopped) - ½ cup
- Green onions (chopped) - 2
- Green bell pepper (chopped) - 1
- Garlic (minced) - 1 clove
- Oil - 2 tablespoons
- Flour - ¼ cup
- Water - 4 cups
- Tomatillos - 1 (7 oz.) can
- Green chiles (canned, chopped) - 2 cups
- Salt - to taste

Instructions

1. Arrange your bed of coals and place the Dutch oven on it.
2. Add the pork and cook until it turns brown.
3. Stir in the onion, green onion, garlic, celery, and bell pepper. Cook until the vegetable become soft, about 10 minutes. Push the mixture to one side of the pot.
4. Add the oil and flour. Stir to form a roux.
5. Stir in the water and the meat mixture. Bring the mixture to a boil.

6. Once the mixture becomes thick, add the green chiles and tomatillos.
7. Stir in salt and simmer for about 30 minutes, or until the meat becomes tender.
8. Garnish with fresh tortillas and serve.

Celery Chili

Total Time: 45 minutes; Prep Time: 10 minutes; Cook Time: 35 minutes
Servings: 6

Ingredients

- Avocado oil - 2 tablespoon
- Ground meat (use turkey, bison, beef, or chicken) - 2 pounds
- Onions (chopped) - 2 cups
- Garlic (minced) - 2 tablespoons
- Red bell pepper (cored, deveined, & chopped) - 1
- Celery (chopped) - 1 cup
- Jalapeño pepper (cored, deveined, & chopped) - 1
- Tomato paste - 2 tablespoons
- Dried oregano - 1/2 tablespoon
- Garlic powder - 1 tablespoon
- Bay leaves - 2
- Chili powder - 4 tablespoons
- Ground cumin - 2 teaspoons
- Fire-roasted diced tomatoes – 24-oz can
- Beef broth - 1 cup
- Salt – to taste
- Pepper - to taste

To Garnish Use:

- Green onions (sliced)
- Yellow onions (chopped)
- Avocado (diced)

- Fresh jalapeño slices

Instructions

1. Add the meat to your Dutch oven and cook over medium heat until it turns brown. Break up the meat and transfer it to a bowl.
2. Add the oil to the pot and heat.
3. Add the onion, jalapeno, celery, garlic, and bell pepper. Cook for about 5 minutes. Stir occasionally.
4. Add the oregano, tomato paste, chili powder, bay leaves, cumin, pepper, and salt. Stir to combine.
5. Stir in the pickled jalapeno juice, beef broth, and diced tomatoes.
6. Return the meat to the pot and bring the mixture to a boil.
7. Lower the heat to medium-low and simmer for about 45 minutes, stirring occasionally.
8. Remove the pot from heat and allow the chili to cool down for about 10 minutes.
9. Garnish with the green onions, jalapeno, avocado, and yellow onions.
10. Serve.

Nutrition Fact

Calories: 512 | Protein: 29g | Carbohydrates: 17g | Fiber: 5g | Sugar: 7g | Fat: 36g

Spicy Hamburger BBQ Beef

Servings: 8

Ingredients

- Beef chuck roast - 2 lb
- Celery (chopped) - 1/2 cup
- Onion (chopped) - 1/2 cup
- Green pepper (chopped) - 1/2 cup
- Water - 1 quart
- Ketchup - 1
- Taco sauce - 3 tbsp
- Brown sugar - 2 tbsp
- Vinegar - 2 tbsp
- Minced garlic - 1 tsp
- Salt - 1 tsp
- Dry mustard - 1 tsp
- Chili powder - 1 tsp
- Bay leaf - 1
- Hamburger buns - 8

Instructions

1. Add the beef, onion, pepper, and celery to your Dutch oven.
2. Cover with water and cook for 2 hour 30 minutes.
3. Remove the meat from the pot and break it into large chunks.
4. Shred the meat and return it back into the pot.
5. Except for the buns, add other ingredients and cook for about 1 hour.

6. Serve over the buns.

Sirloin Steak And Barley Soup

Total Time: 40 minutes

Servings: 4

Ingredients

- Sirloin steak (trimmed & chopped into bite-size pieces) - 8 ounces
- Pepper (freshly ground, divided) - ½ teaspoon
- Extra-virgin olive oil (divided) - 4 teaspoons
- Medium onion (chopped) - 1
- Celery (sliced) - 1 large stalk
- Large carrot (sliced) - 1
- Tomato paste - 2 tablespoons
- Fresh thyme (chopped) - 1 tablespoon
- Quick-cooking barley - ¾ cup
- Low-sodium beef broth - 4 cups
- Water - 1 cup
- Salt - ¼ teaspoon
- Red-wine vinegar - 2 teaspoons

Instructions

1. Sprinkle ¼ teaspoon of pepper on the steak.
2. Add 2 teaspoons of oil to your Dutch oven and heat over medium heat
3. Add the steak to the pot and cook for about 2 minutes, or until it turns brown.
4. Transfer the steak to a bowl and set aside.
5. Add the remaining oil and heat.

6. Stir in the celery and onion and cook for 2 minutes.

7. Add carrot and saute for another 2 minutes. Stir occasionally.

8. Stir in the thyme and tomato paste. Cook and stir for 2 minutes.

9. Stir in the barley, salt, water, broth, and the remaining pepper. Bring the mixture to a simmer.

10. Lower the heat and cook for about 15 minutes.

11. Return the meat back into the pot and heat for 2 minutes.

12. Remove the pot from heat.

13. Stir in the vinegar and serve.

Nutrition Fact

Calories: 273 | Protein: 19.7g | Carbohydrates: 28.6g | Fiber: 4.6g | Fat: 9g

Beefy Mushroom Soup

Total Time: 40 minutes

Servings: 4

Ingredients

- Vegetable oil - 1 teaspoon
- Beef sirloin steak (boneless, trimmed off excess fat & chopped into bite-size pieces) - 12 ounces
- Fresh mushrooms (quartered) - 8 ounces
- Medium onion (chopped) - 1
- Garlic (minced) - 3 cloves
- Balsamic vinegar - 1 tablespoon
- Low-sodium beef broth - 2 (14 ounce) cans
- Diced tomatoes (no-salt-added, not drained) - 1 (14.5 ounce) can
- Dry red wine - ¼ cup (optional)
- Dried Italian seasoning (crushed) - ½ teaspoon
- Fennel seed (crushed) - ¼ teaspoon
- Ground pepper - ¼ teaspoon
- Kale (chopped) - 3 cups
- Fresh green beans (sliced into bite-size pieces) - 1 cup
- Medium yellow bell pepper (chopped) – 1

Instructions

1. Add the oil to your Dutch oven and heat over medium heat.
2. Add the beef to the pot and cook over medium-high heat until it turns brown. Stir occasionally.

3. Transfer the beef to a plate and set aside.
4. Stir in the onion, mushrooms, and garlic. Cook for about 6 minutes.
5. Add the vinegar. Scrape off brown bits from bottom of the pot.
6. Add the tomatoes, broth, wine, pepper, Italian seasoning, and fennel seed. Bring the mixture to a boil.
7. Add the kale, bell pepper, beef, and green beans.
8. Lower the heat, cover pot, and simmer until the beef becomes tender, about 15 minutes.
9. Serve.

Nutrition Fact

Calories: 209 | Protein: 25g | Carbohydrates: 17.1g | Fiber: 5.3g | Sugar: 7.6g | Fat: 5.1g

Chestnut Beef Steak Strips

Servings: 6

Ingredients

- Vegetable oil - 1/4 cup
- Water chestnuts (sliced, drained) - 1 can
- Round steak (cut into ¼" Strips) – 1½ lb
- Beef gravy - 1 jar
- Bell pepper (cut into strips) - 1
- Chow mein noodles (crunchy)
- Mushrooms (sliced) - 1/2 lb
- Salt - 1/2 tsp

Instructions

1. Heat your oven to 350F.
2. Add the oil and heat.
3. Stir in the onion, steak, mushrooms, pepper, and salt.
4. Cook until the meat turns brown. Stir constantly.
5. Drain it and add the gravy and chestnuts.
6. Cover the pot and simmer for about 2 hours. Stir occasionally.
7. Serve with rice and sprinkle the chow mein noodles over it.

Red Wine Lamb Pie

Total Time: 6 hours 15 minutes
Servings: 6

Ingredients

- Olive oil - 3 tablespoons
- Lamb shoulder meat (diced) - 2 lbs
- Salt and pepper - 1 pinch
- Onion (finely chopped) - 1
- Celery ribs (finely chopped) - 2
- Carrots (finely chopped) - 2
- Garlic (finely chopped) – 3 cloves
- Red wine - 1 cup
- Beef stock - 34 ounces
- Bay leaves - 2
- Sprigs thyme - 3
- Rosemary - 2 stalks
- Ricotta cheese - 1 cup
- Large sweet potatoes (peeled & chopped) - 2
- Butter - 1 tablespoon

Instructions

1. Preheat your oven to 300F and season the lamb with a pinch of pepper and salt.
2. Add 2 tablespoons of olive oil in your Dutch oven and heat over medium heat.
3. Add the meat in batches and brown all sides.
4. Remove the lamb meat and add the remaining 1 tablespoon of olive oil.
5. Stir in the garlic, carrots, onion, and garlic. Cook for about 7 minutes.
6. Return the lamb meat back into the pot.
7. Add the red wine and cook for 2 minutes.
8. Add the stock, thyme, bay leaves, rosemary, and pinch of pepper and salt.
9. Bring the mixture to a boil.
10. Cover the pot, place it in the oven, and cook for 6 hours.
11. Transfer the pot to a stove-top.
12. Remove the lid and cook to reduce the sauce by one third.
13. Meanwhile, add water to another pot with a pinch of salt. Bring it to a boil.
14. Add potatoes and cook for about 8 minutes, or until they become tender.
15. Train it and transfer to a bowl.
16. Add 1 tablespoon of butter, pepper, and salt.
17. Turn your grill on.
18. Add ricotta and potato mix to the lamb mixture.
19. Place on the grill and cook about 7 minutes.
20. Serve.

Stuffed Green Pepper And Rice

Total Time: 15 minutes

Servings: 4

Ingredients

- Beef (ground) - 1 lb
- Large onion (chopped) - 1
- Tomato sauce (divided) - 1 (28 ounce) can
- Water (divided) - 1¼ cups
- Garlic & herb salad dressing mix - 1 (1 ounce) envelope
- White rice (uncooked) - 1 cup
- Large green peppers (seeds removed, halved) - 4
- Garlic powder - ¼ teaspoon
- Salt & pepper

Instructions

1. Add the meat and onion to your Dutch oven and brown over medium heat.
2. Add the salad dressing, 1 cup of water, and 1 cup of tomato sauce. Bring the mixture to a boil.
3. Stir in the rice and cover the pot.
4. Remove the pot from heat and allow it to stand for about 5 minutes.
5. Add the remaining water and tomatoes to a baling dish (9 x 13).
6. Place the pepper in the dish and stuff the pepper with the best mixture.
7. Cover it with foil and bake for about 40 minutes at 400F.
8. Add the sauce over and serve.

Chapter 4

POULTRY

Shrimp Andouille Jambalaya

Total Time: 65 minutes

Servings: 10

Ingredients

- Extra virgin olive oil - 2 tablespoons
- Chicken thighs (boneless, skinless) - 1 ½ lbs
- Andouille sausage (chopped into ¼" Slices) - 1 lb
- Large onion (chopped) - 1
- Celery ribs (diced) - 2
- Green bell pepper (diced) - ½
- Red bell pepper (diced) - ½
- Dried thyme - ½ teaspoon
- Dried oregano - ¼ teaspoon
- Sweet paprika - ¼ teaspoon
- Salt - ½ teaspoon
- Cayenne pepper - ¼ - ½ teaspoon (optional)
- Long grain rice - 1½ cups
- Tomatoes (chopped) - 1 (14 ounce) can
- Chicken broth - 2 cups
- Medium shrimp (peeled & deveined) - 8 ounces
- Parsley (chopped) - 2 tablespoons
- Green onions (finely chopped) - 3

Instruction

1. Preheat your oven to 350F.

2. Add the oil to your Dutch oven and heat.
3. Add the chicken and brown both sides.
4. Stir in the onion, bell pepper, andouille, paprika, thyme, cayenne pepper, celery, and oregano.
5. Stir and cook for 5 minutes, or until the onions becomes soft.
6. Add the rice, broth, and tomatoes. Bring the mixture to a boil.
7. Transfer the mixture to a baking dish and top with the chicken.
8. Bake for about 45 minutes, he until the rice is fully cooked.
9. Stir in the parsley, shrimp, and green onions.
10. Cook for about 8 minutes or until the shrimp changes color to pink.
11. Serve.

Chicken Thigh Jambalaya

Total Time: 50 minutes; Prep Time: 20 minutes; Cook Time: 30 minutes
Servings: 4

Ingredients

- Oil (or use bacon grease) - 2 tablespoons
- White onion (diced) - ¼
- Green pepper (diced) - ¼
- Celery (diced) - ½ stalk
- Roasted (crushed tomatoes) - 1 (14oz) can
- Rice - 1 cup
- Sausage (sliced) - 1
- Raw shrimp (peeled & deveined, tail on) - 9
- Chicken thighs (skinless) - 2
- Garlic (minced) - 1 clove
- Paprika - 1 teaspoon
- Cumin - ⅛ teaspoon
- Thyme - 1 spring
- Chicken stock - 1 ⅔ cups

Instructions

1. Add the oil to your Dutch oven and heat over medium-high heat.
2. Add the onion, green bell pepper, celery, sausage, and chicken to the pot and saute for about 3 minutes.
3. Stir in the rice and keep it from sticking by stirring.
4. Add the paprika, garlic, thyme, and cumin. Stir constantly for 2 minutes.
5. Add the chicken stock and tomatoes.

6. Cover the pot and cook for about 10 minutes.

7. Stir in the shrimp, cover, and cook for another 10 minutes.

8. Serve.

Tomato Sopa de Lima

Servings: 8

Ingredients

- Olive oil - 2 tbsp
- Garlic (peeled) - 4 cloves
- Diced tomatoes - 2 cups (up to 5 roma tomatoes)
- Jalapeno (halved & seeded) - 1
- Medium onion (diced, divided) – 1 (about 1 cup)
- Chicken stock - 4 cups
- Lime juice - ¼ cup (up to 4 limes)
- Dried thyme - ½ tsp
- Dried oregano - 1 tsp
- Chicken thighs (boneless, skinless) - 4
- Sea salt
- Black pepper (freshly ground)

Instructions

1. Prepare a bed of coals and place your Dutch oven on top.
2. Add the olive oil to the pot and heat.
3. Add the onion, jalapeno, garlic, salt, and tomatoes. Stir and cook for about 15 minutes.
4. Stir in the chicken. Cook for 5 minutes.
5. Add the thyme, stock, oregano, and salt. Scraoe the brown bits from the bottom of the pot.
6. Bring the mixture to a simmer.

7. Simmer the mixture for about 20 minutes, or until it cooks through.

8. Shred the chicken and adjust seasonings as desired.

9. Garnish with cilantro, onion, tortilla chips, like juice, and avocado.

10. Serve.

Orange Pineapple Chicken

Servings: 8

Ingredients

- Chicken breasts (skinless, boneless, cut in halves) - 4
- Pineapple rings - 8 (~ 1 20-ounce can)
- Clementine orange - 1
- Favorite BBQ sauce - 12 ounces

Instructions

1. Place the chicken breast pieces in your Dutch oven and top each piece with the pineapple ring.
2. Place orange sections in the center of the rings.
3. Pour the pineapple juice and BBQ sauce over.
4. Bake for 45 minutes at 350F.
5. Serve over noodles or rice.

Tarragon Carrot Chicken

Total Time: 40 minutes; Prep Time: 10 minutes; Cook Time: 30 minutes
Servings: 4

Ingredients

- Chicken breast halves (boneless skinless) – 4 (5 ounces each)
- Paprika - 2 teaspoons
- Olive oil - 1 tablespoon
- Julienne carrots - 1 package (10 ounces)
- Fresh mushrooms (sliced) - 1/2 pound
- Condensed cream of chicken soup (low-sodium, undiluted) - 2 cans (10¾ ounces each)
- Dried tarragon - 3 teaspoons
- Lemon juice - 1 tablespoon
- Small zucchini (thinly sliced) – 3

Instructions

1. Sprinkle the chicken with paprika.
2. Add the oil to your Dutch oven and heat over medium heat.
3. Add the chicken and cook each side for about 2 minutes or until it slightly turns brown. Remove the chicken from the pot.
4. Add the mushrooms and carrots to the pot.
5. Cover the pot and cook for about 8 minutes, or until the carrots become crisp-tender. Stir occasionally.
6. Add the tarragon, mix soup, and lemon juice in a bowl and blend well. Pour the mixture over the veggies.

7. Return the chicken back to the pot and bring to a boil.
8. Lower the heat to low, cover pot, and cook for 8 minutes.
9. Add the zucchini on top, cover pot, and cook until the vegetable become tender, about 7 minutes.

Nutrition Fact
Calories: 345 | Protein: 35g | Carbohydrates: 28g | Fiber: 5g | Sugar: 16g | Fat: 11g

Chicken Sausage Okra Gumbo

Total Time: 2 hour minutes; Prep Time: 15 minutes; Cook Time: 1 hour 45 minutes

Servings: 8

Ingredients

- Canola oil - 1/2 cup
- All-purpose flour - 2/3 cup
- White onions (chopped) - 1 cup
- Green bell peppers (chopped) - 1/2 cup
- Celery (chopped) - 1/2 cup
- Garlic (crushed & chopped) - 3 cloves
- Cajun seasoning - 2 tablespoons
- Sausage (smoked, sliced into crosswise) - 8 ounces
- Chicken breast halves (cubed) - 2
- Chicken stock - 5½ cups
- Worcestershire sauce - 1 tablespoon
- Bay leaves - 2
- Rice - 2 cups
- Okra (sliced into crosswise) - 1 cup
- Fresh parsley (loosely packed, chopped) - 1/3 cup

Instructions

1. Mix the oil and flour in your Dutch oven and cook over medium-low hear for about 15 minutes. Stir constantly while cooking.

2. Add the bell peppers, onions, garlic, celery, and Cajun seasoning. Cook for 5 minutes, or until the vegetables become tender. Stir frequently.

3. Add the sausage and chicken and cook for 5 minutes. Stir occasionally.

4. Stir in the Worcestershire sauce, stock, and bay leaves and bring to a simmer.

5. Cook for about 1 hour.

6. Prepare the rice following the package instructions.

7. Add the okra in the gumbo and simmer for 20 minutes, or until the okra becomes tender.

8. Remove from heat.

9. Serve the gumbo with the cooked rice, sprinkled with hot sauce and parsley.

Nutrition Fact

Calories: 773 | Protein: 45g | Carbohydrates: 59g | Fat: 39g

Chipotle Chicken Roasted

Total Time: 1 hour 50 minutes; Prep Time: 20 minutes; Cook Time: 1 hour 30 minutes

Servings: 4

Ingredients

- Whole chicken - 1 (4 lb)
- Chipotle peppers - 2 (+ 2 tbsp of sauce from a can of chipotle in adobo sauce)
- Extra-virgin olive oil - 3 tablespoons
- Sea salt - 1 tablespoon

Instructions

1. Put the chicken in your refrigerator and allow it to refrigerate for 4 hours.
2. Preheat your oven to 450F.
3. Add the adobo sauce, chipotle pepper, and olive oil in your food processor. Pulse for 30 seconds, or until well blended.
4. Rub the mixture under the chicken skin and all over the skin with your finger.
5. Season with salt and use kitchen twine to tie the legs.
6. Break the joints and turn its wings under the breast.
7. Place in the oven and roast for 15 minutes.
8. Lower heat to 300F and roast for additional 70 minutes.
9. Remove from heat and allow it to cool down a bit.
10. Carve and serve.

Nutrition Fact

Calories: 762 | Protein: 58g | Carbohydrates: 2g | Sugar: 1g | Fat: 57g

Chicken And Dumplings

Total Time: 1 hour 30 minutes; Prep Time: 20 minutes; Cook Time: 1 hour 10 minutes

Servings: 8

Ingredients

- All-purpose flour (divided) - 3/4 cup
- Salt - 1/2 teaspoon
- Pepper (freshly ground) - 1/2 teaspoon
- Broiler/fryer chicken (cut up) - 1 (~ 3 pounds)
- Canola oil - 2 tablespoons
- Large onion (chopped) - 1
- Medium carrots (chopped) - 2
- Celery ribs (chopped) - 2
- Garlic (minced) – 3 cloves
- Chicken stock - 6 cups
- White wine (or apple cider) - 1/2 cup
- Sugar - 2 teaspoons
- Bay leaves - 2
- Whole peppercorns - 5

For The Dumplings

- All-purpose flour - 1-1/3 cups
- Baking powder - 2 teaspoons
- Salt - 3/4 teaspoon
- 2% milk - 2/3 cup
- Butter (melted) - 1 tablespoon

For The Soup

- Heavy whipping cream - 1/2 cup
- Fresh parsley (minced) - 2 teaspoons
- Fresh thyme (minced) - 2 teaspoons
- Salt to taste
- Pepper to taste

Instructions

1. Add ½ cup of flour, pepper, and salt to your bowl and mix.
2. Add the chicken to the bowl and toss to coat.
3. Add the oil to your Dutch oven and heat over medium-high heat.
4. Fry the chicken until both sides turns brown. Remove the chicken from the pot.
5. Add carrots, celery, and onion to the pot and cook fir about 8 minutes, or until the onion becomes tender. Stir occasionally.
6. Add the garlic and cook for 1 minute, starring constantly
7. Add ¼ cup of flour and stir until the mixture is well blended.
8. Add the stock gradually and stir constantly.
9. Add the peppercorns, wine, bay leaves, and sugar and stir.
10. Return the chicken to the pot and bring mixture to a boil.
11. Lower the heat and simmer for about 25 minutes, or until the juice becomes clear. Remember to cover the pot.
12. For the dumplings, whisk the baking powder, flour, and salt together in a bowl.
13. Whisk the melted butter and milk together in a separate bowl. Add it to the flour mixture.
14. Stir until it becomes moist. Scoop tablespoonfuls onto a lined baking sheet. Set it aside.

15. Remove the chicken from the pot and allow it to cool.
16. Discard the bay leaves and gently skim fat from the soup.
17. Remove bones and skin from the chicken and shred the meat with forks into 1" pieces.
18. Return the chicken to the soup, cover and cook on high until the soup reaches a simmer.
19. Drop the dumplings on the soup and lower the heat to low.
20. Cover and cook for about 18 minutes, or until the dumplings cooks through.
21. Add the parsley, cream, and thyme and stir
22. Season with more salt and pepper. Serve.

Nutrition Fact

Calories: 470 | Protein: 32g | Carbohydrates: 29g | Fiber: 2g | Sugar: 5g | Fat: 24g

Rosemary And Herb Roast Chicken

Total Time: 1 hour 20 minutes; Prep Time: 20 minutes; Cook Time: 1 hour
Servings: 4

Ingredients

- Whole chicken - 1 (~ 4½ pounds)
- Unsalted butter - 4 tablespoons
- Lemons (halved) - 3
- Thyme - ½ bunch
- Rosemary - ½ bunch
- Salt
- Black pepper (freshly ground)

Instructions

1. Preheat your oven to 425F and use aluminum foil to line a baking sheet. Place roasting rack on the baking sheet.
2. Rinse chicken and use paper towels to pat dry. Bend the wings around the chicken neck.
3. Use your finger and rub the softened butter all over the chicken.
4. Stuff the herbs and lemon inside the chicken.
5. Use kitchen twice to tie the legs.
6. Transfer to the roasting rack and roast for about 40 minutes, or until the chicken turns golden brown
7. Lower heat to 375F and roast until the chicken is fully cooked.
8. Allow the chicken to cool down for about 15 minutes.
9. Carve and serve.

Nutrition Fact

Calories: 616 | Protein: 44g | Carbohydrates: 5g | Sugar: 1g | Fat: 46g

Buffalo Chicken Noodles

Total Time: 1 hour 30 minutes; Prep Time: 20 minutes; Cook Time: 15 minutes

Servings: 8

Ingredients

- Whole-wheat elbow noodles - 12 ounces
- Canola oil - 2 tablespoons
- Medium carrots (sliced) - 3
- Medium celery (sliced) – 3 stalks
- Large onion (chopped) - 1
- Garlic (minced) - 1 tablespoon
- Chicken breast (boneless, skinless, trimmed & chopped into 1" Cubes) - 2 pounds
- Cornstarch - ⅓ cup
- Low-fat milk - 4 cups
- Salt - ⅛ teaspoon
- Hot sauce - 5 tablespoons
- Crumbled blue cheese - 3/4 cup (~ 4 ounces)

Instructions

1. Preheat your oven to 400F.
2. Add water to your Dutch oven and bring to a boil.
3. Add the noodles and cook for about 2 minutes so it doesn't get tender. Drain the noodles, rinse and set it aside.
4. Add the oil to your Dutch oven and heat over medium heat.

5. Add the celery, onion, carrots, and garlic. Cook for about 5 minutes, or until it begins to soften.

6. Add the chicken and cook for about 7 minutes.

7. Whisk the milk and cornstarch in a bowl and pour the mixture in the pot.

8. Add salt and bring to a boil.

9. Cook over medium-high heat for about 4 minutes, or until it becomes thick. Stir frequently.

10. Remove the pot from hear and ass the hit sauce. Stir to mix.

11. Spread the noodles in your baking dish.

12. Add the mixture on top and sprinkle over with the blue cheese.

13. Bake the casserole for about 30 minutes, or until it starts to bubble.

14. Allow it to stand for about 10 minutes.

15. Serve.

Nutrition Fact

Calories: 441 | Protein: 36.9g | Carbohydrates: 47.2g | Fiber: 4.7g | Fat: 12.2g

Braised Leek Turkey

Servings: 6

Ingredients

- Turkey drumsticks (skin-on, bone-in) - 2 (~ 2 pounds)
- Turkey thighs (skin-on, bone-in) - 2 (~ 3 pounds)
- Kosher salt
- Black pepper (freshly ground)
- Olive oil - 1 tablespoon
- Pancetta (chopped to ½" Pieces) - 1/4 pound
- Leeks (only use the white & light green parts, sliced thinly) - 2
- Medium celery stalks (coarsely chopped) - 2
- Garlic (minced) - 3 cloves
- Dry white wine - 3/4 cup
- Fresh thyme - 6 sprigs
- Fresh sage leaves (coarsely chopped) - 1/4 cup
- Bay leaves - 2
- Turkey (or chicken) stock - 2 cups
- Collard greens (leaves chopped with center ribs removed) - 1 large bunch (~ 6 cups)
- Medium sweet potatoes (peeled & chopped into 2" Cubes) - 3
- Apple cider vinegar - 2 tablespoons

Instructions

1. Place a rack in the middle of your oven and preheat to 350F.
2. Pat dry the turkey with paper towels and season with pepper and salt.
3. Add the oil to your Dutch oven and heat over high heat.

4. Add the turkey to the pot and cook each side for about 5 minutes, or until it turns brown.
5. Transfer the turkey to a plate and set it aside.
6. Reduce the heat to medium.
7. Add the pancetta and cook until the meat turns brown. Stir occasionally.
8. Stir in the celery, leeks, pepper, and ½ teaspoon of salt. Cook for about 8 minutes or until it becomes soft.
9. Add the garlic and saute for 1 minute.
10. Add the wine and scrape the brown bits from the bottom of the pot.
11. Cook until the wine reduces by half.
12. Add the sage, thyme, stock, and bay leaves to the pot. Bring to a boil.
13. Add the collard, submerged in the liquid.
14. With the skin side facing up, place the turkey on the collard greens.
15. Bake for about 1 hour and stir in the sweet potatoes.
16. Place the pot on the oven and bake for about 1 hour, or until the meat cooks through.
17. Add the apple cider vinegar and stir.
18. Allow it to stand for about 7 minutes. Serve.

Nutrition Fact

Calories: 817 | Protein: 84.1g | Carbohydrates: 27.8g | Fiber: 6.1g | Sugar: 5.9g | Fat: 38.1g

Garlic Braised Chicken With Soy Sauce

Total Time: 65 minutes; Prep Time: 5 minutes; Cook Time: 60 minutes
Servings: 4

Ingredients

- Extra virgin olive oil - 1 ½ tablespoons
- Chicken leg quarters (trim off excess skin and fat) - 4
- Diced shallots - ¼ cup
- Garlic (thinly sliced) - 4 cloves
- Grated ginger - 1 tablespoon
- Chicken stock - 1 cup
- Low-sodium soy sauce - 1 cup
- Light brown sugar - ½ cup
- White pepper - ¼ teaspoon

To serve use:

- Green onion (thinly sliced) - 2
- Steamed jasmine rice - 3 cups

Instructions

1. Preheat your oven to 350F.
2. Add the oil to your Dutch oven and heat over medium-high heat.
3. Season the chicken with pepper and salt.
4. Place in the oven, with the skin side down, and sear for about 4 minutes. Flip and sear for more 4 minutes.
5. Transfer to a bowl and set it aside.
6. Drain the drippings in the pot and reserve 1 tablespoon of oil.

7. Lower the heat to medium, add garlic shallots to the pot. Saute for 2 minutes.
8. Add ginger and saute for 50 seconds.
9. Deglaze by adding stock. Simmer for about 70 seconds.
10. Add the pepper, soy sauce, and sugar and stir. Simmer for 7 minutes.
11. Return the chicks back into the pot with the skin side facing up and cover the pot.
12. Place the pot in the oven and cook for 40 minutes.
13. Put the cooked rice in your serving bowls and place the chicken on top.
14. Spread the braising liquid over.
15. Top with green onion and serve.

Nutrition Fact
Calories: 696 | Protein: 32g | Carbohydrates: 73g | Fiber: 2g | Sugar: 30g | Fat: 7g

Spicy Chicken Peas Soup

Total Time: 1 hour

Servings: 8

Ingredients

- Extra-virgin olive oil - 2 tablespoons
- Onion (chopped) - 1 cup
- Garlic (minced) - 2 large cloves
- Fresh thyme (chopped) - 1 tablespoon
- Bay leaf - 1
- Low-sodium chicken broth - 8 cups
- Chicken breasts (bone-in, skin removed) - 2 pounds
- Celery (sliced) - 2 cups
- Carrots (sliced) - 2 cups
- Frozen peas - 2 cups
- Salt - 1 ¼ teaspoons
- Ground pepper - ½ teaspoon
- Whole-wheat egg noodles (cooked) - 3 cups
- Fresh parsley (chopped) - ¼ cup

Instructions

1. Add the oil to your Dutch oven and heat over medium heat.
2. Add the garlic and onion. Stir and cook for 3 minutes.
3. Stir in the thyme and bay leaf. Cook for 1 minute.
4. Add the chicken and broth. Cover the pot.
5. Increase the heat to high and bring mixture to a simmer.

6. Uncover and cook for 20 minutes or more, or until the chicken is fully cooked.
7. Transfer the chicken to a cutting board and shred once it cools down.
8. Meanwhile, add the carrots, peas, and celery to the pot. Return the mixture to a simmer.
9. Cook for about 10 minutes.
10. Return the chicken back into the pot.
11. Stir in the pepper, salt, and noodles.
12. Cook for about 4 minutes to heat through.
13. Remove the pot from heat.
14. Stir in parsley and serve.

Nutrition Fact
Calories: 274 | Protein: 26.2g | Carbohydrates: 25.1g | Fiber: 4.8g |
Fat: 7.1g

Chicken Spinach Chili Verde

Total Time: 30 minutes

Servings: 6

Ingredients

- Pinto beans (no-salt-added, rinsed, divided) - 2 (15 ounce) cans
- Canola oil - 1 tablespoon
- Chicken thighs (boneless, skinless, trimmed & chopped into bite-size pieces) - 1 ½ pounds
- Yellow onion (chopped) - 2 cups (1 medium)
- Poblano peppers (chopped) - 2 cups (2 large)
- Garlic (chopped) - 5 cloves (~ 1½ tablespoons)
- Unsalted chicken stock - 4 cups
- Prepared salsa verde - 1½ cups
- Salt - ½ teaspoon
- Frozen corn kernels - 2 cups (about 12 ounces)
- Spinach (chopped) - 2 cups (about 2 ounces)
- Fresh cilantro (coarsely chopped) - 1 ½ cups
- Sour cream - 6 tablespoons

Instructions

1. Add 1 cup of beans to a bowl and mash them.
2. Add the oil to your Dutch oven and heat over high heat.
3. Add the chicken cook for about 5 minutes, or until it turns brown. Stir occasionally.
4. Add the stock, salsa, salt, mashed beans, and the remaining beans.

5. Bring mixture to a boil.
6. Lower the heat to medium heat and simmer for 3 minutes until the chicken cooks through.
7. Stir in the cilantro, corn, and spinach.
8. Cook for about a minute, or until the spinach wilts.
9. Top with the sour cream and serve.

Nutrition Fact

Calories: 408 | Protein: 31.6g | Carbohydrates: 40.5g | Fiber: 8.6g | Fat: 13.9g

Turkey Sausage Okra Gumbo

Total Time: 40 minutes

Servings: 8

Ingredients

- Hot Italian turkey sausage links - 12 ounces
- Canola oil - 2 teaspoons
- Large onion (diced) - 1
- Garlic (minced) - 4 cloves
- Cajun seasoning - 1 teaspoon
- All-purpose flour - 2 tablespoons
- Tomatoes (chopped) - 4 cups
- Reduced-sodium chicken broth - 4 cups
- Frozen chopped okra - 2 ½ cups
- Instant brown rice - ¾ cup
- Scallions (trimmed & sliced) - 1 bunch (optional)

Instructions

1. Add the sausage to your Dutch oven, cook and crumble over medium-high heat for about 5 minutes.
2. Transfer to a bowl and set aside.
3. Add the onion to the pot. Stir and saute for 2 minutes.
4. Stir in the Cajun seasoning and garlic. Cook and stir for 40 seconds.
5. Add the flour and stir for about 1 minute or until it turns brown.
6. Add the tomatoes and stir for 2 minutes.
7. Stir in the chicken broth and cover the pot.

8. Raise the heat to high heat and bring the mixture to a boil.

9. Return the sausage back into the pot.

10. Add the okra and rice.

11. Lower the hear and simmer until the rice becomes tender, about 12 minutes.

12. Sprinkle the scallion slices over it and serve.

Nutrition Fact

Calories: 165 | Protein: 11.5g | Carbohydrates: 17.8g | Fiber: 3g | Sugar: 4.9g | Fat: 6.2g

Chapter 5

SOUPS AND STEWS

Gruyere Onion Soup

Total Time: 7 hours 25 minutes; Prep Time: 5 minutes; Cook Time: 7 hours

Ingredients

- Unsalted butter - 4 tablespoons
- Sweet onions (thinly sliced) - 3
- Garlic (minced) – 2 cloves
- Beef broth - 6 cups
- Brandy - ¼ cup
- Dried bay leaf - 1
- Fresh thyme (chopped) - 2 tablespoons
- Kosher salt
- Black pepper (freshly ground)
- Baguette (cut into ¼" Pieces) - ⅓
- Gruyère cheese (shredded) - 1½ cups
- Fresh chives (chopped) for serving

Instructions

1. Add the butter to your Dutch oven and melt over medium heat.
2. Add the onion to the pot and saute for about 5 minutes.
3. Lower the heat to low and cook for 15 minutes or more until the onions are caramelized.
4. Add the garlic and stir.
5. Transfer the mixture to a slow cooker.
6. Add the brandy, broth, thyme, and bay leaf.
7. Set the slow cooker to low and cook for about 7 hours.

8. Season with pepper and salt.
9. Preheat your broiler.
10. Transfer the mixture into an oven-safe dish.
11. Place 2 slices of the baguette and top with ¼ cup of Gruyère.
12. Broil for 3 minutes until the cheese melts completely.
13. Garnish with the choice and serve.

Nutrition Fact

Calories: 338 | Protein: 16g | Carbohydrates: 26g | Sugar: 10g | Fat: 17g

Bean And Celery Soup

Total Time: 1 hour 15 minutes

Servings: 6

Ingredients

- Extra-virgin olive oil - 1 tablespoon
- Large onion (diced) - 1
- Celery (diced) - 1 large stalk
- Large carrot (diced) - 1
- Water - 9 cups
- Low-sodium chicken broth - 4 cups (32-ounce carton)
- Pearl barley - ½ cup
- Dried black beans - ⅓ cup
- Great northern beans (dried) - ⅓ cup
- Dried kidney beans - ⅓ cup
- Chili powder - 1 tablespoon
- Ground cumin - 1 teaspoon
- Dried oregano - ½ teaspoon
- Salt - ¾ teaspoon

Instructions

1. Add the oil to your Dutch oven and heat over medium heat.
2. Stir in the celery, onion, and carrot, and cook for 5 minutes.
3. Add the broth, water, great northern beans, barley, kidney beans, cumin, black beans, oregano, and cumin. Over high heat, bring the mixture to a simmer.

4. Lower the heat and cook for about 2 hours, or until the beans become tender. Add more water if necessary.

5. Season with the salt.

6. Serve.

Nutrition Fact

Calories: 205 | Protein: 8.8g | Carbohydrates: 36.4g | Fiber: 10.6g | Fat: 3.2g

Fish Cilantro Stew

Total Time: 45 minutes

Servings: 4

Ingredients

- Extra-virgin olive oil - 2 tablespoons
- Medium onion (chopped) - 1
- Garlic (minced) - 4 cloves
- Flaky white fish (chopped into 1½" Pieces) - 1 pound
- Diced tomatoes - 1 (14.1 ounce) can
- Poblano chile pepper (chopped) - 1
- Packed fresh cilantro (chopped) - ¼ cup
- Pimento-stuffed green olives (sliced) - 2 tablespoons
- Capers (rinsed) - 1 tablespoon
- Dried oregano - 1 teaspoon
- Salt - ½ teaspoon
- Water - ½ cup
- Avocado (chopped) - 1 (optional)

Instructions

1. Add the oil to your Dutch oven and heat over medium heat.
2. Add the onion and cook for 4 minutes. Stir occasionally.
3. Stir in the garlic and cook for 1 minute.
4. Ad the chile pepper, fish, olives, oregano, tomatoes, cilantro, capers, and salt. Stir thoroughly to combine. You can add more water if it becomes too thick.

5. Cover the pot and simmer for about 20 minutes.
6. Remove the pot from heat and garnish with avocado.

Nutrition Fact

Calories: 189 | Protein: 20.2g | Carbohydrates: 8.5g | Fiber: 2.4g | Fat: 8.3g

Cauliflower Spinach Soup

Total Time: 1 hour 30 minutes

Servings: 12

Ingredients

- Extra-virgin olive oil - 2 teaspoons
- Onions (chopped) - 2 cups
- Carrots (chopped) - 2 cups
- Garlic (minced) - 4 cloves
- Cumin (ground) - 1 teaspoon
- Coriander (ground) - 1 teaspoon
- Turmeric (ground) - 1 teaspoon
- Cinnamon (ground) - ¼ teaspoon
- Pepper (ground) - ¼ teaspoon
- Vegetable broth - 6 cups
- Water - 2 cups
- Cauliflower (chopped) - 3 cups
- Lentils - 1 ¾ cups
- Tomatoes (diced) - 1 (28 ounce) can
- Tomato paste - 2 tablespoons
- Fresh spinach (chopped) - 4 cups
- Fresh cilantro (chopped) - ½ cup
- Lemon juice - 2 tablespoons

Instructions

1. Add the oil to your Dutch oven and heat over medium heat.

2. Add carrots and onions to the pot and cook for about 10 minutes. Stir occasionally.

3. Add the garlic and stir. Cook for 1 minute.

4. Stir in the coriander, cinnamon, cumin, pepper, and turmeric. Stir and saute for a minute.

5. Add the water, cauliflower, broth, tomatoes, lentils, and tomato paste. Bring the mixture to a boil.

6. Lower the heat and simmer for about 50 minutes, or until the lentils become tender.

7. Add the spinach and stir until it wilts, about 5 minutes.

8. Stir in the lemon juice and cilantro.

9. Serve.

Nutrition Fact

Calories: 151 | Protein: 9.3g | Carbohydrates: 27.5g | Fiber: 9.4g | Sugar: 6.8g | Fat: 1.5g

Spicy Lemon-Celery Chicken Soup

Total Time: 1 hour 15 minutes; Prep Time: 15 minutes; Cook Time: 1 hour
Servings: 8

Ingredients

- Whole chicken - 1 (4-pound)
- Large yellow onion (peeled & cut into large pieces) - 1
- Medium carrots (cut into large pieces) - 2
- Celery (cut into large pieces) – 2 stalks
- Garlic (cut crosswise) – 1 large head
- Jalapeño (cut lengthwise) - 1 (+ more for garnish)
- Ginger (peeled & chopped) - 2 (3-inch) pieces
- Fresh parsley - 1 large bunch (+ more for garnish)
- Coriander seeds - 1 tablespoon
- Kosher salt - 1 tablespoon
- Black pepper (freshly ground) - 2 teaspoons
- Fresh spinach - 6 ounces (170g)
- Lemons (thinly sliced) – 2

Instructions

1. Add the chicken, carrot, jalapeno, onion, ginger, garlic, coriander, celery, black pepper, parsley, and salt to your Dutch oven and combine.
2. Cover the mixture with enough cold water.
3. Cover the pot and bring the mixture to a boil over high heat.
4. Lower the heat to low, cover the pot, and simmer for about 1 hour or until the chicken becomes tender.

5. Transfer the chicken to a bowl and strain the stock into a saucepan. Keep the stock warm over low heat.
6. Shred the chicken and place in your serving bowls with spinach, lemon slices, and jalapeno.
7. Top with the hot broth and serve.

Nutrition Fact

Calories: 387 | Protein: 31g | Carbohydrates: 12g | Sugar: 3g | Fat: 24g

Black Bean Coconut Soup

Total Time: 35 minutes; Prep Time: 10 minutes; Cook Time: 25 minutes
Servings: 6

Ingredients

- Vegetable oil - 2 tablespoons
- Large onion (chopped) - 1 (~ 2 cups)
- Scallions (sliced, with the green parts reserved) - 3
- Garlic (minced) – 5 cloves
- Fresh thyme leaves - 1 teaspoon
- Scotch bonnet - ¼
- Kosher salt - 1 teaspoon (plus extra)
- Black pepper (freshly ground) - ¼ teaspoon (plus extra)
- Allspice - ¼ teaspoon
- Chicken stock - 2 cups (plus extra)
- Black beans (drained & rinsed) - 2 (15-ounce) cans
- Unsweetened coconut milk - ½ cup (plus extra for garnish)
- Fresh lime juice - 1 tablespoon
- Jalapeño slices - to serve

Instructions

1. Add the oil to your Dutch oven and heat over medium heat.
2. Add the scallions, thyme, onion, garlic, pepper, bonnet, and salt. Cook for about 8 minutes. Stir occasionally.
3. Stir in the allspice and cook for 1 minute.

4. Add the coconut oil, stock, and beans. Bring mixture to a simmer over medium-high heat. Lower the heat to a simmer. Cook for 15 minutes.
5. Transfer the mixture to your food processor or blender and blend until it becomes smooth.
6. Return the soup to the pot. Add the like juice and stir.
7. You can add more stock to get your desired consistency, and adjust seasoning to taste.
8. Garnish with coconut milk, scallion greens, and jalapeno slices.
9. Serve.

Nutrition Fact

Calories: 268 | Protein: 12g | Carbohydrates: 34g | Sugar: 4g | Fat: 10g

Chickpea Tomato Soup

Total Time: 30 minutes

Servings: 8

Ingredients

- Olive oil - 1 tablespoon
- Medium red onion (chopped) - 1
- Garlic (minced) – 4 cloves
- Jalapeno peppers (seeded and chopped) - 2 (optional)
- Pepper - 1/4 teaspoon
- Vegetable broth - 8 cups
- Red quinoa (rinsed) - 1 cup
- Chickpeas (no-salt-added, rinsed, and drained) - 2 cans (15 ounces each)
- Black beans (no-salt-added, rinsed, and drained) - 1 can (15 ounces)
- Medium tomatoes (chopped) - 3
- Fresh corn - 1 cup
- Fresh cilantro (minced) - 1/3 cup

Optional Ingredients

- Crushed tortilla chips
- Cubed avocado
- Lime wedges
- Extra chopped cilantro

Instructions

1. Add the oil in your Dutch oven and heat over medium-high heat.

2. Add the garlic, red onion, pepper, and jalapeno. Cook and stir for about 5 minutes.

3. Stir in the quinoa and broth. Bring mixture to a boil.

4. Lower the heat and simmer for 10 minutes until the quinoa becomes tender.

5. Stir in the beans, corn, chickpeas, cilantro, and tomatoes.

6. Cook to heat through.

7. Serve with the other optional ingredients.

Nutrition Fact

Calories: 289 | Protein: 13g | Carbohydrates: 48g | Fiber: 9g | Sugar: 5g | Fat: 5g

Goat Cheese Tomato Soup

Total Time: 1 hour 45 minutes; Prep Time: 30 minutes; Cook Time: 1 hour 15 minutes

Servings: 10

Ingredients

- Fresh tomatoes (halved) - 1¾ pounds
- Sweet onion (peeled & quartered) - 1
- Garlic - 1 head
- Olive oil - ¼ cup
- Salt
- Black pepper (freshly ground)
- Chicken broth - 3 cups
- Bay leaf - 1
- Thyme - 2 sprigs
- Fresh basil (chopped) - 3 tablespoons
- Crumbled goat cheese - ⅓ cup

Instructions

1. Preheat your oven to 375F and use aluminum foil to line your baking sheet.
2. Place the tomatoes, garlic, and onion on the baking sheet and drizzle oil over.
3. Season with pepper and salt.
4. Roast for about 40 minutes, or until the tomatoes begins to blister.
5. Squeeze out the garlic clove, add it to your Dutch oven.

6. Add the tomatoes and garlic to the pot.
7. Stir in the thyme, bay leaf, and broth. Bring to a simmer.
8. Simmer for about 25 minutes over medium-low heat.
9. Transfer the mixture to your food processor and blend until mixture becomes smooth.
10. Ladle into serving bowls.
11. Garnish each bowl with 2 tablespoons of goat cheese and 1 teaspoon of basil.
12. Serve.

Nutrition Fact

Calories: 90 | Protein: 2g | Carbohydrates: 6g | Sugar: 4g | Fat: 7g

Ribollita Soup

Total Time: 40 minutes; Prep Time: 10 minutes; Cook Time: 30 minutes
Servings: 6

Ingredients

- Dried white beans (washed, soaked for 3 hours) - 1 pound/500 g
- Small onion (peeled & chopped) - 1
- Small carrot (peeled & chopped) - 1
- Celery (chopped) - 1 (6-inch) stalk
- Small bunch parsley (flat-leaf, chopped) - 1
- Olive oil - 1/4 cup
- Tomato paste - 1½ tablespoons
- Kale (removed ribs, leaves chopped) - 1 pound/500 g
- Beet greens (removed ribs, leaves chopped) - 1 pound/500 g
- Potatoes (peeled & diced) - 1/2 pound/250 g
- Sea salt
- Black pepper (freshly ground)
- Fresh thyme - 1 sprig
- White bread (day-old crusty Italian, thinly sliced) - 1/2 loaf

Instructions

1. Add the beans to a pot and cover it with water by about 2 inches and boil. You can add more water to keep it submerged. Add small salt when it's almost done.
2. Add the oil to your Dutch oven and heat.
3. Add the onion, parsley, celery, and carrot. Saute for about 8 minutes.

4. Add the cooking liquid from the beans and the tomato paste.
5. Stir in the beet greens, kale, and potatoes.
6. Add the beans and stir well.
7. Season with pepper, salt, and thyme.
8. Simmer for about 15 minutes, or until the potatoes become tender.
9. Discard the thyme.
10. With the sliced bread, arrange in alternating layers with the soup and serve.

Nutrition Fact

Calories: 435 | Protein: 22g | Carbohydrates: 67g | Fat: 11g

Spicy Potato Soup

Total Time: 40 minutes

Servings: 4

Ingredients

- Extra-virgin olive oil - 2 tablespoons
- Large onion (diced) - 1
- Hot paprika - 3 teaspoons
- Vegetable broth - 2 (14.1 ounce) cans
- Medium plum tomatoes (diced) - 4
- Medium yellow summer squash (diced) - 1
- Diced cooked potatoes - 2 cups
- Green beans (chopped into 2" Pieces) - 1½ cups
- Frozen spinach - 2 cups (5 ounces)
- Sherry vinegar - 2 tablespoons
- Fresh basil (chopped) - 1/4 cup

Instructions

1. Add the oil to your Dutch oven and heat over medium heat.
2. Add the onion and cook for about 6 minutes until it browns. Stir occasionally.
3. Stir in the paprika and cook for 30 seconds.
4. Add the broth, squash, beans, tomatoes, and potatoes. Bring mixture to a boil.
5. Lower the heat to simmer and cook for about 12 minutes, or until the veggies become tender.

6. Stir in the vinegar and spinach, and cook to beat through, about 3 minutes.
7. Transfer to your serving bowl and top with the basil.

Nutrition Fact

Calories: 244 | Protein: 8.8g | Carbohydrates: 37.7g | Fiber: 9.5g | Fat: 8.3g

Tortellini Turkey Sausage Soup

Total Time: 35 minutes; Prep Time: 20 minutes; Cook Time: 15 minutes

Servings: 8

Ingredients

- Italian turkey sausage links (removed casings) - 3
- Medium onion (chopped) - 1
- Garlic (minced) – 4 cloves
- Red pepper flakes (crushed) - 1/4 teaspoon
- Low-sodium chicken broth - 6 cups
- Pasta sauce - 1 jar (24 ounces)
- Crushed tomatoes - 1 can (15 ounces)
- Tomato paste - 2 tablespoons
- Dried basil - 2 teaspoons
- Balsamic vinegar - 2 teaspoons
- Dried parsley flakes - 1 teaspoon
- Sugar – 1½ teaspoons
- Dried oregano - 1/2 teaspoon
- Salt - 1/4 teaspoon
- Pepper - 1/2 teaspoon
- Frozen cheese tortellini - 2 cups
- Parmesan cheese (shredded) optional

Instructions

1. Add the sausage and onion to your Dutch oven and cook over medium heat for about 7 minutes, or until the sausage changes color.

2. Crumble the sausage and drain.

3. Stir in the pepper flakes and garlic. Cook for 1 minute.

4. Add the pasta sauce, broth, tomato paste, crushed tomatoes, vinegar, parsley, basil, oregano, salt, sugar, and pepper. Stir and bring the mixture to a boil.

5. Add the tortellini and cook for about 5 minutes. Stir occasionally.

6. Serve, topped with cheese.

Nutrition Fact

Calories: 192 | Protein: 12g | Carbohydrates: 26g | Fiber: 4g | Sugar: 12g | Fat: 5g

Rice, Beef, And Vegetables Soup

Servings: 12

Ingredients

- Olive oil
- Ground beef - 3 lb
- Cayenne pepper - 1 tsp
- Garlic powder - 2 tbsp
- Dry onion soup mix - 1 pkg
- Vegetable soup - 2 (10-oz.) cans
- Vegetable-beef soup - 2 (10-oz.) cans
- Onions (diced) - 2
- Rice - 2 cups
- Water - 4 cups

Instructions

1. Add the beef, onion, soup mix, cayenne pepper, and garlic powder.
2. Grease your Dutch oven with oil and heat to 350F.
3. Form ½" meatballs with the beef mixture.
4. Place the meatballs in the pot and fry.
5. Remove the oil in the pot.
6. Add the cans of vegetable soup.
7. Add the rice, onions, and water. Bring mixture to a boil.
8. Stir in the meatballs and cover the pot.
9. Lower the heat to 225F and simmer for about 20 minutes, or until the rice is fully cooked.

Roasted Tomato Soup

Total Time: 50 minutes; Prep Time: 20 minutes; Cook Time: 30 minutes
Servings: 8

Ingredients

- Olive oil - 1 tablespoon
- Medium onion (chopped) - 1
- Celery (sliced) - 1 stalk
- Medium carrot (chopped) - 1
- Bottled minced garlic - 1 teaspoon (2 cloves)
- Low-sodium chicken broth - 3 (14.5 ounce) cans
- Butternut squash (cubed, peeled) - 2 cups
- Diced tomatoes (fire-roasted) - 1 (14.5 ounce) can
- White kidney beans (rinsed, drained) - 1 (15 ounce) can
- Small zucchini (halved lengthwise and sliced) - 1
- Small broccoli - 1 cup
- Snipped fresh oregano (crushed) - 1 tablespoon
- Salt - ¼ teaspoon
- Black pepper (freshly ground) - ¼ teaspoon
- Freshly shredded parmesan cheese - 1 pinch

Instructions

1. Add the oil to your Dutch oven and heat over medium heat.
2. Add the onion, carrots, celery, and garlic. Cook for 5 minutes.
3. Stir in the squash, broth, and tomatoes. Bring mixture to a boil.
4. Lower the heat, cover pot, and simmer for about 20 minutes.

5. Add the zucchini, salt, beans, pepper, oregano, and broccoli. Cook for extra 5 minutes.
6. Sprinkle with the Parmesan cheese and serve.

Nutrition Fact

Calories: 92 | Protein: 5.7g | Carbohydrates: 16.1g | Fiber: 3.8g | Fat: 2g

Cabbage Potato Stew

Servings: 4

Ingredients

- Potatoes (diced) - 3
- Carrots (diced) - 3
- Cabbage (shredded) - 1/4 head
- Celery (diced) - 3 stalks
- Smoked sausage (cut into 1" Pieces) - 1 lb
- Lemon pepper - 1/8 tsp
- Black pepper - 1/8 tsp
- Water

Instructions

1. Add all ingredients to your Dutch oven and mix.
2. Cover with enough water.
3. Cook for about 2 hours over coal, or until it is fully done.
4. Serve

Chapter 6

BREADS AND DESSERTS

Huggies Biscuit

Ingredients

- Hershey kisses - 1 bag
- Cooking oil - 1 bottle
- Pillsbury biscuit dough - 1-2 packages
- Powdered sugar - 1/2 cup

Instructions

1. Put the sugar in a ziploc bag.
2. Add the oil to your Dutch oven and heat to 375F.
3. Wrap the Hershey Kiss in the biscuit dough.
4. Add it to the pot and cook until it turns brown.
5. Remove from the pot and allow it to cool.
6. Add it to the ziploc bag and shake.

Spicy Mustard Sausage

Servings: 8

Ingredients

- Polish sausage - 4 lbs.
- Onions (sliced) - 2
- Brown sugar - 2 cups
- Spicy brown mustard - 1/2 cup
- Garlic (minced) – 4 cloves
- Water - 1 cup
- Ground cayenne pepper - 1/2 teaspoon

Instructions

1. Add the onions and sausage to your Dutch oven.
2. Add other ingredients to a bowl and mix thoroughly.
3. Pour the mixture over the sausage. Stir to combine.
4. Bake at 350F for 1 hour. Stir every 15 minutes.

Beans, Burger, And Biscuits

Ingredients

- Lean hamburger - 2lb.
- Baked beans - 2 (2lb.) cans
- BBQ sauce - 1 cup
- Cheddar cheese (shredded) - 1 cup
- Ketchup - 1/2 cup
- Mustard - 1/2 cup
- Small onion (chopped fine) - 1
- Bisquick mix

Instructions

1. Heat your Dutch oven to 325F.
2. Add the hamburger and cook until it browns.
3. Stir in the beans, BBQ sauce, mustard, ketchup, and onion.
4. Cover the pot and bake at 275F for about 15 minutes.
5. Meanwhile, prepare the bisquick mix to make 12 biscuits.
6. Stir the mixture in the pot and cover it with the biscuits.
7. Sprinkle over with the cheese and cover the pot.
8. Bake until the biscuits are fully cooked, about 30 minutes.

Black-eyed Peas And Ham

Servings: 8

Ingredients

- Bacon slices - 8
- Small onion (chopped) - 1
- Minced garlic - 3 tbsp
- Water - 4 cups
- Shelled black-eyed peas - 6 cups
- Jalapeno pepper (chopped) - 1
- Black pepper - 1/2 tsp
- Cooked ham (chopped) - 1 cup
- Green onions (chopped) - 1/4 cup

Instructions

1. Add the bacon to your Dutch oven and cook at 350F until crisp.
2. Transfer the bacon to a bowl and set it aside.
3. Add the garlic and onion to the pot and saute for 5 minutes.
4. Stir in the black pepper, water, jalapeno, and peas. Bring the mixture to a boil.
5. Cover the pot, lower the heat and simmer for about 65 minutes.
6. Add the ham, bacon, and green onions.
7. Cook for additional 15 minutes.
8. Serve.

No Knead Sourdough Bread

Total Time: 1 hour 5 minutes; Prep Time: 15 minutes; Cook Time: 50 minutes

Servings: 12

Ingredients

- Warm water - 1 1/2 cups
- Instant yeast - 2 teaspoons
- Honey - 1 tablespoon
- All-purpose flour - 5 cups
- Kosher salt - 1 tablespoon
- Plain Greek yogurt - 1 cup

Instructions

1. Add the yeast, water, flour, honey, yogurt, and salt in the bowl of your stand mixer.
2. Use the dough hook or wooden spoon to mix until the flour is well incorporated.
3. Cover with plastic wrap or wet towel for 2 hours or until it doubles in size. Do this at room temperature.
4. If you ant to have a stronger sourdough flavor, put the covered bowl of dough in your fridge and allow it to sit overnight.
5. With a floured surface, form a ball with the dough and transfer it to a lined parchment 4 quart.
6. Let it rise and double in size for about an hour.
7. Preheat the oven to 475F.

8. Bake for about 25 minutes, covered.
9. Uncover and bake for additional 30 minutes, or until the bread turns golden brown.
10. Remove the pot from the oven and transfer the bread to a rack. Allow it for about 2 hours to cool completely.
11. Enjoy.

Cinnamon-Raisin Cornbread

Servings: 8

Ingredients

- Sugar - 1/4 c
- Cinnamon - 1 tsp
- Ground ginger - 1/2 tsp
- Salt - 1/4 tsp
- Nutmeg - 1/4 tsp
- Powdered milk - for 4 cups of water
- Cornmeal - 1/2 c
- Raisins - 1/2 c
- Oil - 2 tbs
- Eggs - 2
- Pancake syrup - 1/2 cup

Instructions

1. Add the sugar, ginger, nutmeg, cinnamon, and salt in a Ziploc bag and mix.
2. Add 4 cups of water in a pot and heat to warm.
3. Stir in the powdered milk and heat to steam.
4. Add the cornmeal and lower the heat to simmering.
5. Stir and simmer until it thickens, about 10 minutes.
6. Remove the pot from heat.
7. Add the egg and oil to a cup and mix well.
8. Add the mixture to the cornmeal and stir.

9. Stir in the raisins, sugar mixture, and syrup.

10. Grease your Dutch oven with oil and pour the mixture into it.

11. Cook at 350F for about 40 minutes.

Candied Cherry And Apple

Serves: 1

Ingredients

- Apple (cored) - 1
- Raisins - 1 oz.
- Brown sugar - 1 tbsp
- Cherry - 1
- Pineapple ring – 1

Instructions

1. With the stem side facing up, place the apple in your Dutch oven.
2. Stuff the core holes with the raisins and brown sugar.
3. Place the pineapple ring on the apple and top it with the cherry.
4. Pour the pineapple juice over and cover the pot.
5. Bake for about 30 minutes at 350F.

Italian Cheese Pizza

Total Time: 30 minutes; Prep Time: 10 minutes; Cook Time: 20 minutes
Servings: 8

Ingredients

- Frozen pizza dough (thawed) - 1 pound
- Olive oil - 1 tablespoon
- Marinara sauce - 1 cup
- Shredded Italian cheese blend - 1 cup
- Bulk spicy pork sausage (cooked and drained) - 8 ounces
- Onion (chopped) - 1/3 cup
- Fresh mushrooms (sliced) - 1/2 cup

Optional:

- Minced fresh basil
- Red pepper flakes
- Parmesan cheese (grated)

Instructions

1. Preheat your oven to 450F.
2. Place your Dutch oven at the bottom rack and heat for about 3 minutes.
3. Roll the dough on a floured surface to make a 12" circle.
4. Make a sling with 18" piece of foul by folding it lengthwise into thirds.
5. Remove the pan from heat and place the dough on the sling.
6. Lower the dough into the pan with the sling left in the pan. Move the dough into place with your spoon.
7. Brush the dough with the oil and spread the marinara sauce on top.
8. Top with the cheese, onion, sausage, and mushrooms.

9. Bake for about 20 minutes, or until the crust turns brown. Allow to cool.

10. Remove from the Dutch oven and serve with red pepper flakes, Parmesan cheese, and basil.

Nutrition Fact

Calories: 273 | Protein: 11g | Carbohydrates: 27g | Fiber: 1g | Sugar: 1g | Fat: 13g

Chocolate Cherry Cake

Total Time: 40 minutes; Prep Time: 5 minutes; Cook Time: 35 minutes
Servings: 8

Ingredients

- Cherry pie filling - 1 can (21 ounces)
- Evaporated milk - 1 can (12 ounces)
- Chocolate cake mix - 1 package
- Sliced almonds - 1/3 cup
- Butter (melted) - 3/4 cup
- Vanilla ice cream (optional)

Instructions

1. Preheat your oven to 350F.
2. Line your Dutch oven (4-quart) with parchment and spray lightly with cooking spray.
3. Mix the evaporated milk and pie filling together and spread the bottom of the Dutch oven with the mixture.
4. Sprinkle the cake mixture and almonds, and drizzle over with the butter.
5. Cover and bake for about 40 minutes, or until the cake springs back whenever it's touched.
6. You can serve with ice cream.

Nutrition Fact
Calories: 515 | Protein: 7g | Carbohydrates: 68g | Fiber: 3g | Sugar: 44g | Fat: 24g

Biscuit And Pot Pie

Servings: 6

Ingredients

For The Biscuits:

- All-purpose flour - 1 1/2 cups
- Sharp cheddar cheese (shredded) - 1/2 cup
- Fresh thyme leaves (chopped) - 1 tablespoon
- Baking powder - 1 1/2 teaspoons
- Kosher salt - 1/2 teaspoon
- Cold heavy cream - 1 cup (+ 3 tablespoons)

For The Pot Pie:

- Olive oil - 2 tablespoons
- Medium yellow onion (chopped) - 1
- Garlic (minced) - 2 cloves
- All-purpose flour - 3 tablespoons
- Low-sodium chicken broth - 2 cups
- Whole milk - 1 cup
- Shredded chicken (cooked) - 3 cups
- Frozen peas and carrots - 1 (10-ounce) package
- Kosher salt - 3/4 teaspoon
- Black pepper (freshly ground) - 1/4 teaspoon

Instructions

1. To make the biscuits, place the rack in the middle of your oven and heat to 425F.

2. Add the flour, baking powder, cheese, salt, and thyme in a bowl and whisk together.
3. Add the cream and stir until it forms a shaggy dough. Place it in your refrigerator.
4. Add the oil to your Dutch oven and heat over medium-high heat.
5. Stir in the onion and cook for about 4 minutes, until it becomes tender.
6. Add the garlic and saute for a minute.
7. Stir the flour and cook until it dissolves. Stir constantly.
8. Stir in the milk and chicken broth. Bring the mixture to a boil.
9. Lower the heat and simmer for about 8 minutes, or until it becomes thick. Stir constantly.
10. Remove the pot from heat.
11. Stir in the peas, chicken, carrots, pepper, and salt.
12. Divide the dough into 6 equal portions and form ½" thick patties with them.
13. Place the patties on the chicken mixture.
14. Bake for about 18 minutes or until the biscuits turn golden brown.
15. Allow it to cool for bout 7 minutes. Serve.

Nutrition Fact

Calories: 623 | Protein: 26g | Carbohydrates: 44.8g | Fiber: 4.9g | Sugar: 9g | Fat: 38.2g

Rose-Raspberry Jam

Servings: 2

Ingredients

- Raspberries - 2 pounds
- Sugar - 1½ cups
- Fresh lemon juice - 1 tablespoon
- Rose water - ¼ teaspoon

Instructions

1. Add the sugar and raspberries to your Dutch oven, toss, and allow it to sit for 30 minutes.
2. Cook the mixture over medium heat for about 40 minutes or until it thickens. Stir frequently.
3. Remove the pot from heat. Stir in the rose water and lemon juice.
4. Transfer to jars, cover, and allow it to chill.

Pecan Chocolate Brownies

Servings: 8

Ingredients

- Flour - 2 c
- Baking powder - 1 tsp
- Baking soda - 1/4 tsp
- Salt - 3/4 tsp
- Butter - 1¼ sticks
- Brown sugar - 2 c
- Eggs - 2
- Vanilla - 2 tsp
- Chocolate chips - 3/4 c
- Chopped pecans - 3/4 c

Instructions

1. Add the flour, baking soda, baking powder, and salt to a Ziploc bag and mix.
2. Add the butter to a pot and melt.
3. Add the butter, vanilla, and eggs. Mix well.
4. Stir in the flour mixture and mix.
5. Once the mixture becomes smooth and thick, transfer it to your Dutch oven.
6. Sprinkle over with the pecans and chocolate chips.
7. Cover the pot and bake at 350F for about 20 minutes.
8. Serve.

Tangy Cabbage With Onion & Apple

Total Time: 2 hours 5 minutes; Prep Time: 20 minutes; Cook Time: 1 hour 45 minutes

Servings: 4

Ingredients

- Butter - 4 tablespoons
- Large onion (quartered and sliced) - 1
- Large tart apple (peeled, cored, and diced) - 1
- Cabbage (shredded) - 1/2 head (~ 8 cups)
- Black pepper - 1/4 teaspoon (freshly ground)
- Cider vinegar - 3 tablespoons
- Apple jelly - 1/4 cup
- Kosher salt

Instructions

1. Add the butter to your Dutch oven and melt over medium-low heat.
2. Stir in the onion and apple. Cook for about 7 minutes until the onion becomes soft.
3. Add the black pepper, cabbage, vinegar, and the jelly. Stir thoroughly to combine.
4. Cover the pot and simmer for about 1 hour 30 minutes over low heat.
5. Add salt to taste.

Nutrition Fact

Calories: 236 | Protein: 5g | Carbohydrates: 32g | Fat: 12g

Taco Tomato Dip Platter

Total Time: 1 hour 50 minutes; Prep Time: 20 minutes; Cook Time: 1 hour 30 minutes

Servings: 20

Ingredients

- Ground beef - 2 pounds
- Large onion (chopped) - 1
- Diced tomatoes (not drained) - 1 can (14½ ounces)
- Tomato paste - 1 can (12 ounces)
- Tomato puree - 1 can (15 ounces)
- Chili powder - 2 tablespoons
- Ground cumin - 1 teaspoon
- Garlic powder - 1/2 teaspoon
- Salt - 2 teaspoons
- Ranch style beans - 2 cans (15 ounces each)
- Corn chips - 1 package (9¼ ounces)
- Hot cooked rice - 2 cups

For The Toppings

- Cheddar cheese (shredded) - 2 cups
- Medium onion (chopped) - 1
- Medium head iceberg lettuce (shredded) - 1
- Medium tomatoes (chopped) - 3
- Ripe olives (sliced, drained) - 1 can (2¼ ounces)
- Picante sauce - 1 cup (optional)

Instructions

1. Add the beef and onion to your Dutch oven and cook over medium heat until the meat changes color.
2. Add the following 7 ingredients and cover.
3. Simmer fir about 1 hour 30 minutes.
4. Add the beans and cook until it heats through.
5. Layer the rice, corn chips, cheese, meat mixture, onion, tomatoes, lettuce, and olive.
6. Serve with the picante sauce.

Nutrition Fact

Calories: 522 | Protein: 27g | Carbohydrates: 47g | Fiber: 8g | Sugar: 9g | Fat: 24g

Walnut Chocolate Cobbler

Servings: 8

Ingredients

- Chocolate cake mix - 1
- Cherry pie filling - 1 can
- Soda pop - 1 can
- Chocolate bar - 1
- Walnuts (chopped) - optional

Instructions

1. Place the pie filling in a pie tin.
2. Layer ¾ of the chocolate cake mix on top.
3. Pour in ½ can of the soda and stir into the cake mix layer.
4. Cut the chocolate bar into pieces and place them on top.
5. Sprinkle the walnut on top.
6. Place the tin in your Dutch oven. Use pebbles on the bottom of the pot for support.
7. Bake at 350F for about 40 minutes, or until the cake is done.

Layered Taco Beef Pie

Servings: 6

Ingredients

- Ground beef – 1½ lb
- Taco sauce - 8 oz.
- Large corn tortillas - 4
- Cheddar cheese (shredded) - 8 oz.
- Tomato puree - 8 oz.

Instructions

1. Preheat your Dutch oven to 325F.
2. Mix the tomato puree and taco sauce together.
3. Add the beef to the pot and cook until it turns brown. Remove it from the pot and drain.
4. Add 2 of the tortillas to the pot, topped with ½ of the beef.
5. Spread half of the taco mixture on the beef.
6. Add half of the taco mixture and top with 2 tortillas.
7. Pour the rest of the beef followed by the taco sauce.
8. Sprinkle over with the cheese.
9. Cover the pot and bake until the cheese melts completely.

Creamy Egg Berry

Total Time: 40 minutes; Prep Time: 15 minutes; Cook Time: 25 minutes
Servings: 6

Ingredients

- Butter - 1/2 cup
- Eggs - 9
- Milk - 1½ cups
- Vanilla - 1 tablespoon
- Lemon zest – 1 lemon
- Flour - 1½ cups
- Salt - 1/2 teaspoon
- Berries - 4 cups
- Powdered sugar - 1/4 cup
- Lemon juice to squeeze on berries (optional)

Instructions

1. Prepare up to 24 charcoals.
2. Add the eggs, vanilla, milk, and lemon zest to a bowl and mix.
3. Whisk in the flour along with the salt until the mixture blends.
4. Make a bed if 8 coals and place your Durch oven on top.
5. Add the butter and melt completely.
6. Add the batter and cover the pot.
7. Place the remaining coals on the pot lid.
8. Cook for about 25 minutes until it sets.
9. Remove the pot from heat.

10. Add the powdered sugar, berries, and lemon juice.

11. Close the pot and allow the berries to get warm.

12. Cut and serve.

Nutrition Fact

Calories: 439 | Protein: 14g | Carbohydrates: 40g | Fiber: 3g | Sugar: 12g | Fat: 24g

9 781667 122267